The Winning Touch in Golf

THE WINNING

TOUCH IN GOLF

A PSYCHOLOGICAL APPROACH

By **PETER G. CRANFORD, Ph.D.**

With an introduction by
CARY MIDDLECOFF

Illustrated by
Lealand Gustavson

BRAMHALL HOUSE · NEW YORK

The author wishes to express his grateful appreciation to Mrs. Randolph L. Fenninger for her generous typing and editorial assistance, and to Dr. William S. Boyd for his critical reading of the manuscript.

This edition is published by Bramhall House,
a division of Clarkson N. Potter, Inc.,
by arrangement with Prentice-Hall, Inc.
(B)

The Winning Touch in Golf, by Peter G. Cranford, Ph.D.

© MCMLXI by Prentice-Hall, Inc.

Library of Congress Catalog Card Number 61-15087

Printed in the United States of America 73227-T

To my wife Helen
Who Knows the Psychological Secrets of How to Keep a
Golfing Husband Happy

Introduction:

THIS BOOK CAN BE THE START
OF YOUR GOLFING IMPROVEMENT

by
Cary Middlecoff

Nobody who has ever thought about the game of golf seriously can doubt that the psychological factors involved are tremendous. Certainly I have never doubted it. On the contrary, I have often wished—yearned, even—for a better and deeper understanding of this science of the mind as it applies to golf and golfers.

These moments of yearning have come when, head in hands, I sought earnestly but vainly to explain to myself how I had missed a short putt or a simple shot that I knew myself physically capable of making. The wishing for greater knowledge of golf psychology goes on continually, because I know my overall golf game would be better if I had it.

For a graphic and familiar example of the importance of psychology in golf, we have readily at hand in the records the vividly contrasting performance of Arnold Palmer on the 72nd and last hole of the 1960 and 1961 Masters Tournaments. In 1960, you will recall, this great competitive golfer came to the last hole needing a birdie three to win the tournament by a stroke over Ken Venturi. He made it with a strong and accurate drive, a masterfully played six-iron shot to within six feet of the pin, and a smoothly and resolutely stroked putt that was, as the saying goes, in all the way.

Add to this 1960 picture these further facts: Palmer had, in fact, reached the 71st hole needing two birdie threes to win, and he was perfectly aware of what the situation demanded, Venturi having finished about half an hour earlier, with no one else in contention except these two. So here we have a man of iron nerves, impervious to "pressure."

Then a year later to the day, this same Palmer reaches the same hole of the same tourament needing only a par four to win. A bogey five, moreover, will give him a tie and the chance to win by beating Gary Player the following day in a playoff. Again he hits a strong and straight drive, but instead of the great finish of a year before, he plays out the hole as a 95-shooter might and takes a double-bogey six to lose.

Did Palmer in 1961, as many unthinking people later suggested, yield to "pressure?" Nonsense. How could he have? He was a year richer in experience, and many thousands of dollars richer in money. Additionally, he had won the tournament before, as had not been the case a year earlier, and any competitive golfer will tell you that it's easier to win a big tournament the second time than it is the first, from the standpoint of so-called pressure.

What was it then? I can't explain it, but I'm sure the answer lies in the realm of psychology, just as the answers to the otherwise inexplicable failures and successes of yours and mine in golf lie in the realm of psychology. Palmer was psychologically "right" in 1960 and psychologically "off" in 1961.

But psychology enters into golf long before the player reaches the last hole in a tight and dramatic situation. In fact, it pervades the game. It is vitally important in the learning process, beginning with the time the aspiring golfer picks up his first club. It remains vitally important in all of the practice, in all the day to day informal games, and carries through any tournament play the golfer may undertake.

All this being so, it is surprising that the subject has been so little explored up until now. The answer here may lie in the fact that, as I once observed in my own instructional golf writing, that a writer-golfer-psychologist is a rare combination.

However rare the combination, we have it now in Dr. Peter G. Cranford, Ph.D. That he is a writer, and a good one, is evident on every page of this book. Beyond that, and perhaps surprisingly for a scholar of Dr. Cranford's attainments, he is a writer of remarkable clarity and simplicity. Reading his book will not necessitate having a dictionary at hand for frequent consultation. Neither will it be necessary that the reader himself be steeped in the lore of psychology. Dr. Cranford makes it abundantly clear that his message is to fellow golfers—not to his colleagues in psychology—and the message comes through loud and clear.

Dr. Cranford's credentials as a golfer are established early in his book and supported by documentary evidence throughout. His own meticulously and assiduously kept records show him to be a player who scores in the 70s with some consistency, which is plenty good. But not alone in records does he show himself to be a dedicated, devoted golfer. Virtually every paragraph tells you that here is a man who plays golf, thinks golf, lives golf. What diletante golfer, for instance, would practice thousands of putts on his living room rug so as to be able to assess the value of "carpet putting practice?"

The author's standing as a psychologist is, of course, attested to by his degree and his long experience in the field. That he turned this study and experience to the subject of golf is a break for all of us.

In my judgment, Dr. Cranford does most for the golfer who aspires to lower his score when he writes on the general subject of learning through practice. It has been my observation that most golfers start out a golfing season with high hopes and firm determination to get better through practice, but allow themselves to become discouraged too quickly and slip back into the old ruts. Such chapters as "How to Overcome Inertia," "How to Make Time and Place Work For You," and "How to Avoid Conditions That Kill Interest" will cut strokes off many a golf score.

The great beauty of this book is that the author has had the interest and the patience to accumulate a vast knowledge about the learning process of golf by making trial-and-error experiments and recording the results. He is thus able to state with authority which learning methods are apt to work and which are not worth the time and effort. Through this alone, a reading of his book can save any golfer untold frustrations and set him on the right path to learning the game.

His chapter on "How to Handle Anger" will, of course, be more valuable to the temperamental than to the placid, but there is hardly a golfer who will not derive a considerable benefit from it.

But here is the book for you to read. The first chapter is entitled "How To Begin To Improve," and I suggest that a good way to begin to improve is begin immediately to read this book. My firm prediction is that you will find in it expert confirmation of some ideas you have had about the psychology of golf, plus a great many new ideas which you can put into practice with profit.

You may feel after reading *The Winning Touch In Golf*, as I did, that perhaps the most valuable secret that Dr. Cranford imparts about golf is the game's fascination for its devotees regardless of age or ability. Dr. Cranford, like a certain other Dr. whose teeth I brush each morning, has been playing the game of golf for several decades. Yet both of us are still dog-gedly trying to achieve some mastery of the game.

We have both had some success and a lot of pleasure out of golf, as well as a lot of the disappointments that serve to heighten the pleasure of the successes when they come. Both of us know that neither of us will ever know all the secrets of the game, and both of us realize that in this fact lies the great appeal of golf.

Many of the secrets, though, the good Georgia doctor has revealed. I expect to apply a number of them beneficially, and so can you.

Preface

The objective of this book is to reduce your scores as quickly as possible, by teaching you to apply simple principles of the science of psychology. Throughout the history of golf, there has been much *said* about the important part that psychology plays in the game, but very little has been *written*. Cary Middlecoff brought this deficiency to public attention recently, and suggested that the remedy might have to await the work of someone with experience in both golf and psychology.

It has been my good lot to have had this experience over a period of more than 25 years. My primary interest in psychology has always been in how it could be applied, not only in my clinical work with patients, but also in other pursuits that could be made more profitable, more efficient or more pleasurable.

This is not a theoretical book. The material has been accumulated over a quarter of a century, and has been derived from notes taken while I was playing or practicing. Whenever I saw that an application of psychology to golf produced results, I recorded it. As a consequence, I think the reader will find that the suggestions are practical. If followed, they will produce a lowering of scores.

How low your scores become will depend largely upon your persistence. Persistence has been historically described as the secret of success, but this is not always true. We must have persistence which is properly directed. It is my hope that such proper direction is provided by this book.

Peter G. Cranford

Table of Contents

The Winning Touch in Golf

1st, SECRET

How to Begin to Improve

The first secret of golf betterment is an emotional one. *You must have or develop the desire to improve.* The strength of this "want" will determine one's persistence, and persistence is the secret of success. Fortunately, the reader has already demonstrated his desire to improve, or he would not have bothered to read this far.

The desire to improve should be strengthened by being based upon strong needs. Great interest can thus be generated. Great interests produce other interests, which in turn produce others, like the branches, twigs, and leaves of a tree.

Years ago, I had a patient whose emotional illness had caused him to lose interest in everything. He had been ill so long that all his funds were exhausted. During the process of his therapy, one of the problems facing him was how to rechannel his morbid thinking into something more constructive. He had by now recovered enough to want an interest but had not the financial means to exploit the usual avenues of recreation. One day, as he left the office, he absent-mindedly plucked some leaves from a bush. When he found them in his hand, he realized that

2

he not only did not know how they got there but he also had no idea what they were. It flashed through his mind that here was something he could do to begin to develop an interest in life, and he determined to learn the name of each shrub between the office and his home. This he did. It involved much more time and research than he expected, but when the job had been done, he had developed a permanent interest in plant life. Today he is happy and well, teaching botany as a profession and deriving additional income from his hobby as a nurseryman.

Ed Furgol, Bobby Cruickshank and others took up golf originally for reasons of health, and they can give testimony to the additional stimulus given to the development of interest when it grows out of real needs.

These needs are not necessarily physical in origin. One of our great needs is what has been called "personality plus." This means that most individuals are made happier if there is one area of their lives in which they rise above their fellow man. People seek this "personality plus" in hundreds of ways—collecting cigar bands, swallowing gold fish, or the seeking of skills in competitive games. Of all the outdoor games, golf now seems best able to provide the "personality plus" with the most additional benefits. Two of these benefits, emotional and physical health, are the foundation without which life becomes meaningless.

For those who do not have the time, knowledge, or combination of talent and opportunity required to achieve the "personality plus" of championship golf, great satisfaction can be obtained from local renown or from achievement in one of golf's many specialties. Joe Kirkwood, Sr. and Paul Hahn became trick shot artists. It is not too difficult to become locally known as an excellent putter, or as a specialist with a particular club, if a person will devote even as little as fifteen minutes a day to specialized practice. To aim at local recognition is a very satisfactory objective and, if achieved, means much more emotionally than does much greater recognition among strangers.

For those who have the highest ambitions, the undiscouraged young, the want to improve must be long-lasting. It cannot be discouraged by either minor or great defeat. It must be strong enough to endure much sacrifice. It must be concentrated. It cannot concern itself with the desire to achieve greatness in a variety of games. It must concern itself with the development of a passion for correct practice. Nothing will be lost because of great effort, for ultimately the final reward is suitably large, and the effort itself produces many pleasures along the way.

2nd, **SECRET**

You Must Capitalize

upon Past Experience

It was a source of irritation to me in high school geometry when the teacher insisted that we figure each proposition out for ourselves. Many of my classmates memorized the proof, but I tried conscientiously to arrive at the answer. As a consequence my grades were not what they should have been. My final conclusion was that if it took civilization some million years to discover that parallel lines cut by another line had certain peculiarities, I could not be expected to discover them overnight for myself.

The same is true of golf. *A great deal of time can be saved if we absorb what is already pretty well known about the game.* Each generation of golfers is better than the preceding one because use is made of the experiences of those who have come before us. Hence the individual can speed up his mastery of the game by sticking close to present orthodox form. A description of this form is the stock in trade of the professionals, and should be acquired from them. It is true that there are good golfers who profess never to have taken a lesson, but most of these have been good imitators. Further, there are hundreds of thousands who have not taken lessons who are still duffers, and thus are not in a position to boast. There is no greater frustration in golf than to find out, ten years too late, that a golfing flaw could have easily been corrected by a competent professional. All would be well advised to seek the services of one, and to stick to him until what he had to teach had been absorbed. This does not mean that many lessons should be taken *ad infinitum.* Fewer lessons, spaced so that ample time is allowed for the learning to sink in, is the better way.

In addition, it is an excellent idea to obtain all the visual instruction one can. This can come from a study of still pictures, or films, or from observing professional golfers, particularly when they are practicing. Written instruction from golf books and magazines is also valuable, provided it is followed by the objective observation of your professional. Otherwise, a misconception of what the author intended will bring about a confusion in your golf learning. It has taken golf 500 years to develop the modern grip, stance, and swing. It is the height of folly not to take advantage of these discoveries.

In the early stages of lesson taking, it is advisable to spread the instruction time over many parts of the game. If, for instance, you had the good fortune to be able to take a series of lessons from someone of the calibre of Arnold Palmer, it would be best to obtain instruction in all broad aspects of the game, such as might be obtained from a playing lesson. Generally speaking, it has been found that learning is tied together much better if one goes through the whole process than if he learns it piece by piece. This should be followed up with considerable practice before the next lesson. By "considerable," we would mean at least a thousand shots each for woods, irons, chips, and putts.

3rd, **SECRET**

Why Practice Is a Necessity

The greatest pleasure in golf comes from continuous improvement. This can only come about through correct practice. For those who aspire to creditable play, practice is doubly necessary. "Creditable play" implies a competitive element, in that one's ability becomes "creditable" if it is more skillful than that of others. Other things being equal, the practicer has the advantage.

In general, the great practicers have led the field. This is a comparatively recent development in golf. Although much prac-

WHY PRACTICE IS A NECESSITY

ticing was done by a few individuals prior to the modern era, it was generally believed that golfing ability was rather like musical talent and that it could not be acquired by concentrated, conscious effort. In fact, during the twenties, many professionals thought that practice beyond a good warm-up might even be injurious.

The change in attitude was first heralded in the golfing world by the phenomenal success on the American circuit in the '30's of Torchy Toda. His excellent play was a reflection of the determination of the Japanese government to obtain world recognition in sports. The first step was to select from their young men those who seemed to have golfing talent. Instructors were imported from the United States. Practice was instituted as a full-time daily procedure. At the end of only two years, Japan had produced golfers of world renown. Among American golfers, the practicing trend seems to have been started by Henry Picard. A generation ago he practiced iron play from dawn to dusk, until he achieved such confidence with second shots to the green that he confessed to Orville White that he had the feeling that each shot might go into the hole. I had the opportunity to see him in practice prior to play in an open tournament at Thomasville, Georgia. His shots with a four iron were so accurate that the caddy hardly moved a step in catching balls on the first bounce. I have seen only one other golfer with such accuracy with irons—the greatest practicer of them all—Ben Hogan. It is significant that Picard was Hogan's closest golfing friend. Hogan's meteoric rise convinced the golfing world that, even though good golfers might be *born*, it was also possible to *make* oneself good. The story is told that on one occasion when Hogan sought the advice of a prominent professional, his swing was so unimpressive that he was advised to abandon the game. The substance of Hogan's answer was that the would show him.

We now have "practicers" in great profusion. Golf achievement at the highest level is virtually impossible without it. It is a necessity at the amateur level even if one's ambitions are relatively modest.

Since this is true, it is to the advantage of the would-be champion gradually to build up the length of his practice sessions. If he is aiming high, the amount should compare favorably with the hours found necessary in other sports or enterprises involving expert use of muscles. Many singers, violinists, pianists, and other musicians must devote several hours to practice each day, year in and year out. Ice-skating, the ballet, basketball, dancing—in short, anything that involves the training of muscles to a high degree of expertness requires daily practice over a considerable period of time.

Since much of the time in the playing of a round is consumed with walking, talking, and waiting, very little can be learned by playing 18 holes. In a par round of 72, there are 14 drives, perhaps 4 other wood shots, 18 iron shots, and some 36 chips and putts. This requires a time investment of about 4 hours. During practice, a similar number of shots can be hit in 30 minutes. It is thus considerably less time-consuming to learn through practice than through play.

There are some golfers who have become good players without devoting much time to concentrated practice. However, if their golfing career is examined, it will generally be found that they did considerably more *playing* than the average person. It must be admitted that, shot for shot, one can learn more golf by *playing* 85 separate shots in a round than by *practicing* an equal number. This must be true psychologically because, in playing, we are "practicing" precisely the shots the game requires, whereas when we putt on the practice green there is the great danger that we are not duplicating true "playing" conditions. Still, if we are careful to practice the shots called for in the analysis of our mistakes, much more can be learned in four hours of practice than in four hours of play.

The ideal would be to have four hours of practice that exactly duplicated four hours of play. I know of an amateur who did almost precisely this. He lived in a city that had a municipal course which was not kept in good shape, and hence rules about practice were non-existent. The golfer got two caddies, eighteen balls, and an electric golf cart. For 30 mornings prior to the tournament he was entered in, he played eighteen balls for nine holes. In the tournament he made the best showing of his golfing career.

What practice can accomplish is indicated by the following: I have heard of two instances of exceptionally good first rounds. One young lady shot an 85 from men's tees on a demanding course. She had taken lessons and practiced for two years before ever going out on the links. A young man who had a job at a driving range shot a 76 on a standard course on his first round, after having practiced for a little more than a year. It is not likely that either one of them would have done nearly as well if the same amount of time had been spent in play that was 99% waiting and walking and 1% hitting the ball.

One of the earliest of the hard practicers was Joe Kirkwood, Sr. who, in the 1920's, concentrated on trick shots. This was still the day of the stymie, when it was occasionally necessary to hop over an opponent's ball to make a putt. At four feet, Joe Kirkwood could use a lofted club and put the ball in the hole on the fly!

Although Betsy Rawls, the great woman golfer, is endowed with considerable natural talent, much of her success is due to her early attitude toward practice. While the rest of us would be playing at the old Austin Country Club, she would take her habitual stand under a tree on the 13th hole and hit balls by the hour. It was only on rare occasions that she would play with us, even though she was already the equal of most male golfers. Before we realized it, she was an Open Champion.

4th, **SECRET**

How to Overcome Inertia

The next secret of golf is to *overcome inertia*. Muscles have a mind of their own, and do not like to make any move unless impelled to do so. Once they begin to move, the muscles do not seem to care. We must harness this tendency in ourselves to continue doing what we are doing, and may have to take rather sly means of shifting our actions toward practice. Once shifted, the muscles, like Newton's law of motion, prefer to continue golfing unless acted upon by some outside force. This is what we mean by overcoming inertia.

Some people have trained themselves to do, without procrastination, whatever must be done. These people have no problem with inertia. Most of us have to "use psychology" to get ourselves going. In my younger days, I decided that I wanted to build a house with my own hands. Each day I had great difficulty getting started. I asked an old carpenter how he managed to get to work without hesitation. He told me that he once had the same trouble and cured himself.

"How?" I asked.

He replied, "Pick up *something*."

12

When I was in college we were instructed on how to overcome inertia in buckling down to necessary study. We were given essentially the same advice. "Open the book."

I was once engaged in doing tedious research and writing on the history of an old mental hospital. I had the duty of organizing a psychological staff for the hospital and, as a preliminary step, I felt it necessary to know the background of the institution. At that time, I was the only psychologist on the staff, and we had more than 10,000 patients. By supper time I was pretty tired, and it was most difficult for me to stir up any enthusiasm for the history. I succeeded in getting the job done by tricking myself into it. I would say, "I will walk to the office after supper, but I will not go in." When I had gotten that far, I continued with, "I will go in but I won't do any work." The next step was, "I will get my data sheets out, but I will not do any writing." Finally, I told myself, "I will write one paragraph and quit." I finished the manuscript eventually and it proved very useful in developing plans for the hospital. I have derived more personal satisfaction from this unknown effort than from those which attracted more attention and were more profitable financially.

An engineer I knew in Austin, Texas, told me he always had all the professional business he wanted but his big problem was "getting started." Finally, he hit on an idea. He would jot down everything he knew about the project. He did not care how irrelevant the information was to the problem of design. He found that when he had done this, out of the welter of useful and useless information, the design of the project would begin to take shape and the next thing he knew he was actively translating his ideas to the drawing board.

In south Georgia, farmers grind sugar cane in what amounts to an over-size coffee grinder. A horse pulls a lever arm around and around until the day's work is over. On occasions when there is no work to be done, it is not unusual for the horse or mule to leave the barn at the usual hour, go to the sugar mill, and begin nudging the lever arm. If the arm is out, he will begin plodding his circular path. Although a number of interesting morals could be derived from this expression of obsessiveness, it it is enough for us to note its application to the overcoming of inertia.

I rather enjoy practice, but there are occasions when I do not particularly feel like it. This may occur after a lay-off due to unavoidable circumstances. I am able to seduce myself into beginning by saying, "I will practice five minutes and then quit." I have yet to quit after I once get on the practice tee and, in addition, I invariably enjoy the session—even in uninviting weather.

5th. SECRET

How to Make

Time and Place Work for You

After inertia has been overcome, *attention should be directed toward modifying your environment so that learning is automatically stimulated by your surroundings.* The earlier this is done, either by accident or design, the more learning will take place.

This accounts for the fact that good golfers have historically developed from two groups: caddies who from necessity were immersed in a golfing environment, and players with the means and the time to become so immersed.

Although the average amateur cannot modify his environment as thoroughly as these two groups, his golf can be insured a more or less automatic improvement if he will do as much as he can to place himself in a situation that makes it easier for him to play and practice.

It is not an accident that the greatest golfers have developed in areas in which the climate was advantageous, and that many of them lived in close proximity to courses. For several years I deliberately lived close to a driving range, and I feel sure that this accounts for the fact that I am more accurate with woods than with irons. I have always tried to live close to a range or golf course.

In addition to living as closely as possible to golfing facilities, it is wise to *make a permanent provision for play or practice time*. It has been found that a college student does not have trouble buckling down to work if he has a special time and place for study. At the designated hour, strong habits take over, and almost like a robot, he goes to the "study place." Once in the "study place," he pulls out a book; then other habits take over and the work is done automatically. One can build up a series of automatic actions so that long and arduous work can be done without straining to stick to the job.

Let me illustrate in a simple way how you can make environment put you to work. For years I had the problem of not being able to keep the putter blade straight. Too many putts were either cut or pulled. I bought a putting gadget which enabled me to practice on the rug. Experience taught me how easy it was to lose interest in practicing, so I took several precautions. First I placed the putting gadget in a spot where I often saw it —near a dresser in the bedroom. Then I kept a supply of balls in a dresser drawer. I bought a duplicate putter and placed it next to the gadget as an additional reminder, also avoiding the problem of having to go to the bag for a club. I kept a prominently displayed score sheet to see how many out of each hundred putts were dropping. Finally, I made it a habit to putt just before going to bed.

Years ago, when my game was in the middle and high eighties, I had little time for play and had a good bit of trouble hitting tee shots. I had no car at the time and the bus took me from the city to the place where I roomed. Not too far from the bus line was a driving range. Although this range was only a few blocks from where I lived, I did not take full advantage of the opportunity offered. I then made a decision, essentially a psychological one, which led to the straight tee shot. I found a room situated so that the range was between the bus line and the house. Each day when I got off the bus I had to pass the range to get to my living quarters. It became very easy to establish the habit of hitting a bucket or two before going home. This solved the problem by making my environment work for me.

The above are rather commonplace suggestions and are given merely to highlight what can easily be overlooked: that *you must place yourself in a situation which will give your wants a definite place and time to find expression.* Although we are all handicapped by various unfortunate duties, there is still much that can be done to provide better golfing situations without affecting what the world has come to believe are more important things.

6th, **SECRET**

How to

Accelerate Emotional Drive

The characteristic approach to the game by those who succeed involves a fixity of purpose which comes from emotional drive. The drive comes from what psychologists call "goal tensions," and this goal tension comes from the decision of the player to disregard the possible pleasures of the moment for the pleasures of final important achievement. However, the strength of this decision is apt to fluctuate from time to time and, to avoid its weakening, there are ways by which our drive can be further stimulated by conscious effort. Here are some of those methods:

1. *Watch expert golfers in action.* You will tend to identify with them, as you do with the hero in a movie, and as you do so, emotions of various kinds will be aroused which will stimulate your ambitions. After any tournament there is always a great flurry of golfing activity. The golf matches now being portrayed on television will result in even greater golfing interest.

2. *Play in golf tournaments.* A big emotional incentive comes out of competition. People learn much faster if their efforts are competitively successful. They experience an exhilarating lift to

18

which they can easily become addicted. On the other hand, if they lose, their pride is stung and they may be stimulated to redeem themselves through a better showing.

3. *Take lessons from someone you admire.* Many a person has developed a lifelong desire to improve his game by the accident of having been around a person he liked who was a good player. It is not necessary to wait for such an accident to occur. Seek out the professional that you most admire and pay him whatever it costs for lessons. The ideal pro would be one who could both teach and play and also had personal qualities which would serve as a long-range source of stimulation. An example of such a relationship is that between Ken Venturi and Byron Nelson. It may well explain why Venturi is an obsessive practicer.

4. *Consider golf as a stepping-stone to material success.* Golf has developed into big business and, in this business, there are many opportunities. Good playing can lead to money-making on a much larger scale than many other fields. This accounts for the fact that college players with promise are turning down other careers to take their chances on the circuit. Many golfers do exceedingly well in selling clubs and other accessories. Some use connections developed on the golf course as an entree to profitable business deals. A good or even creditable game is a help in both business and social situations. If one becomes a professional even in a comparatively small way, he will find that the returns are good. In some cases, the returns approach the fabulous.

5. *Consider golf as an aid to good health.* Many physicians consider golf the ideal exercise as a promoter of good emotional and physical health. Without excessive strain, it enables one to exercise every muscle in the body. In addition, it promotes mental health by taking the mind off problems which produce emotional stress.

6. *Be a "poor loser."* It is not good psychology to cultivate an attitude of being satisfied with failure. Such an attitude is

self-destructive, since it destroys the emotional drive that is required for sustained effort. Tommy Bolt was so heavily criticized for his angry reactions to poor shots and poor rounds that he set about to completely suppress his feelings. He said later that he quit winning the minute he started becoming a "good loser." I have known several amateurs whose games have deteriorated under similar circumstances.

This does not mean that one must be obnoxious in order to perform at his best. As is mentioned elsewhere in this book, our emotions can be directed into productive channels which will drive us to improve. It has been reported that Bobby Jones in his prime had unpleasant physical reactions during the stress of competition. In the best sense, this great sportsman was a "poor loser."

7th, SECRET

How to Avoid
Conditions that Kill Interest

When I was a freshman at college, our class was given a talk on recreation. The speaker gave us advice which has proved itself so sound in my case that I would advise young men to heed it. He urged us to select hobbies that we could engage in for the balance of our lives. I chose bowling, chess and golf. They have worked out very well for me as a permanent solution to the problem of recreation. One of the additional advantages of the selection was that I did not disperse my learning over many games.

There are a number of conditions which can weaken our interests. Here are precautions you should take:

1. *Avoid competing games.* There is still a great deal of truth in the old adage: "Jack-of-all-trades, master of none." You can obtain a great deal more satisfaction out of a fair degree of excellence in one sport than from poor skill in a number of them. Constant poor showings will produce unnecessary feelings of inferiority.

2. *Avoid false discouragement.* The best way of doing this is to keep records of all practice and play, so that you know precisely what your present level of skill is. Most golfers who become discouraged do so unnecessarily. A golfer who keeps records knows that practice inevitably brings about improvement—even with poor methods. As Harvey Penick once said, "You can learn to hit the ball with any method." Of course, our aim is to improve as fast as we can through sound methods of practice, but the point I wish to emphasize here is that golfers can injure their chances of improvement by becoming defeatists.

On this point, the psychologist William James,[1] presents an argument that is as apropos to golf as it is to education.

"Let no youth have any anxiety about the upshot of his education, whatever the line of it may be. If he keeps faithfully busy each hour of the working day, he may safely leave the final result to itself. He can, with perfect certainty, count on waking up some fine morning to find himself one of the competent ones of his generation, in whatever pursuit he may have

[1] James, William: *Psychology*, page 150, World Publishing Company, Cleveland, Ohio, 1948.

singled out. Silently, between all the details of his business, the *power* of *judging* in all that class of matter will have built itself up within him as a possession that will never pass away. Young people should know this truth in advance. The ignorance of it has probably engendered more discouragement and faint-heartedness in youths embarking on arduous careers than all other causes put together."

False discouragement (discouragement not based on facts) can also grow out of placing oneself in a position that invites defeat. Repeated defeats depress the ego. Unless a person can balance these with a series of repeated successes, he will become unnecessarily discouraged.

Here are a few practical ways to avoid false discouragement:

1. Do not play habitually with better golfers unless the handicaps are such that you win as often as you lose.

2. Do not limit yourself to players who always outdrive you.

3. Do not increase your betting when you will have to come from behind to win.

4. Do not bet against poorer golfers if they demand handicaps which will insure their winning.

5. Do not attempt shots which you do not have in your bag.

6. Do not turn in a better qualifying score than you actually shoot. It is better psychologically to win in a lower flight than to lose in a higher one.

7. Do not concede any putts to yourself or your opponent that can be missed. Discouragement arises from the fact that in a tournament in which all putts must be holed out, you may *think* you are playing badly, when in reality you are playing your regular game.

8. Do not "pull against" your opponent. A series of good

or lucky shots on his part will make a defeatist of you. It is healthier to expect him to play well. If he misses or has tough luck, it will be so much gravy.

9. Do not play with persons who increase your anxiety.

3. *Avoid anxiety and worry in your personal life.* The worries that arise from the process of everyday living affect golf. In virtually all cases, something can be done about them. Since such worries generally result in illness and financial loss, it is cheaper in the long run to seek help from a competent psychologist or psychiatrist. Most people make the mistake of taking unhappiness for granted.

4. *Avoid false pride.* Many people will not seek emotional help from a psychologist or psychiatrist because they consider it a sign of weakness. But in this area, as in golf, it is a much greater weakness to have so much false pride that one cannot take advantage of the superior skills of others. Years ago many golfers had such false pride about instruction. Even today, some writers occasionally encourage such an attitude indirectly by emphasizing that a given player "has never had a lesson." I do not doubt that there are such players, but their judgment is questionable. Most good golfers are anxious to help those with less skill. The golfer with the sort of false pride that prevents him from seeking help can waste years discovering what someone else can give him in a few minutes.

8th, **SECRET**

Stimulate Interest

Through Your Own Golf Crowd

An enduring method of obtaining maximum satisfaction out of golfing, which in turn creates maximum interest, is to *have your own golf crowd*. Some people are emotionally unable to "get up a game," and very often their interest dies out because of false ideas of rejection—a sort of self-pity that develops because they are not always invited to play.

It is not wise to leave golfing friends to chance. They should be deliberately sought. The pleasures of golf, like happiness, are not created merely because we wish them to appear. Then once the crowd is organized, or you become part of one, the persons in it should become more important than the game. They will be quick to sense such an attitude, and the mutual respect that develops is one of the more rewarding aspects of golf. This respect has a tendency to turn into friendships which seem to be much closer and longer-lasting than those in other fields. It is not unusual for foursomes to maintain their ties for more than a quarter of a century. One golfing crowd at the Augusta Country Club known as the "Big Crowd" has a history older than the golfing span of its oldest members—and is still going strong. Their knowledge of each other is so intimate that golf occurrences of apparently slight significance produce banter comparable to well-liquored family reunions.

A further advantage of having one's own crowd is the opportunity it affords for stimulating competition. Interest is developed most when the competition is greatest and the odds are fairest. By betting on the outcome, you will enjoy winning and hate losing. This will help to goad you into a desire for improvement. There is no moral problem involved in reasonable betting, since over a period of time the amount won and lost will be about the same.

It is advantageous to belong to more than one group and, if possible, to a group on another course. This lends variety to play, and variety will prevent your interest from dying out. The maintenance of this interest is necessary not only for your golf, but also to satisfy your requirements for varied recreation.

People of approximately equal ability will tend to gravitate toward each other, so that the problem of whom to play presents no great difficulties. As a golfer becomes better, his circle of golfing friends tends to become limited to good players. This has some dangers, since the pressure is to play with them more than with good companions. If one plays with only those in his class he will find that the game loses much of its pleasures, which can lead to a loss of interest. Personally, I prefer good personalities to good golfers, and many of my most enjoyable rounds have been played with relative "dubs." The ideal is to find the best combination available but, when in doubt, settle for companionship. You can always spot the opposition enough to make an even match.

However, regular playing with good golfers is advantageous for the development of good form. We have seen this occur as an outcome of play on the modern golf circuit. Professional golf has added a great deal to our knowledge of the game because of the rapid exchange of information between experts. It is a similar condition which produces the quickest advances in the scientific field. Without scientific journals and scientific conventions, progress is very slow and difficult. We now have a

condition in which golf experts are in a permanent "convention," and the successful secrets of one soon become the open property of all. To a more limited degree this occurs in smaller amateur groups such as the "steady" foursomes, and play is thereby improved. In addition, obvious deviations of form can be spotted by other members of the group more easily than one can spot them in himself.

9th, SECRET

**How to Stimulate
Interest Through Self-Competition**

An enduring method of insuring continuous progress is to stimulate interest by competing against yourself in practice. There are a number of ways in which this can be done.

1. *With putts:* Putting practice on the average practice green is very tiresome, primarily because so few shots are hit in comparison with the length of time one is on his feet in playing one ball from cup to cup. A method I have found to be more effective is to practice when there are few people around. Select a hole which does not give a level putt and scatter 25 balls around the cup at a distance of about seven feet. This will

come close to duplicating putting conditions as they actually are on the course. You will have straight putts down hill, straight putts up hill, all gradations of putts breaking from left to right, all gradations of putts breaking from right to left, and all the effects of grain. Jot on a score card the number made out of each 100. Then transfer these numbers to a chart which will enable you to strike an average after each 1000 putts. Compete against these scores. Interest never lags and improvement is inevitable.

2. *With chips:* Use a bag of 50 balls. First play them all to the nearest cup on the practice green. Jot on a score card how many result in "gimme" putts. Then play to the second nearest cup, and so on to each cup from that particular position. The next day move in the opposite direction around the green. After you have made a complete circuit, strike a percentage. Then repeat the process, competing against your former scores.

An alternative method which takes a little more time but has a number of psychological advantages is to combine chipping with putting. Use nine of your best balls. Chip to the nearest hole, then sink the ensuing putts. Every two holes constitutes a round. Aim at getting a par of 36. The distance to the hole should be varied each time. It will surprise you to see how many chip shots will drop, and you will also be surprised at how many of the short putts will turn out to be quite difficult. The practice of putting and chipping in combination is the fastest method I know to lower scores. It is also a good way to keep your game from deteriorating if you do not have time to play full rounds very often.

3. *With wedges:* Beginning ten yards from the green, drop balls in a straight line away from the green at intervals of about a yard. Each shot is thus a little longer than the one before. Keep moving away from the green until you reach the distance at which the club is no longer effective. With wedges, either strike averages as before or note how many consecutive shots

you make that leave you with a reasonable putt to finish the hole. With the latter system, if you want a short practice session, stop as soon as you hit five consecutive perfect shots—and then move on to practice with another club. You could extend the series to ten, or could practice until you broke your record for such shots.

4. *With irons:* With other clubs, move back from the green, again dropping balls at yard intervals or less. Keep a record of how many shots out of each 100 are hit to the putting surface.

5. *With woods:* Since there are generally 14 drives on the average 18-hole course, keep records to see how many of each 14 practice shots are good playable drives. When you arrive at a point where you can hit 14 consecutive drives in a row, you know that you cannot lose very many strokes off the tee.

10th, **SECRET**

How to Use

Variety to Maintain Interest

When the same muscles are used continuously in the same fashion, fatigue results. With fatigue there comes a loss of interest. This creates more fatigue. The same is also true if the same thought pattern is continuously repeated. *If we vary our physical and psychological approach to the game, interest can be maintained at a high pitch.*

Hogan states that after he had reached the point in his practice at which he could hit straight shots with regularity, he introduced variety to maintain his interest. He would hit one shot to the left of the caddy, drop one short, lob one just over his head, fade one, hook one, etc. There are also other ways of achieving variety, such as hitting shots of the same length with different clubs.

Variety can be introduced by playing strange courses or by playing with a different golf group. Experimenting with problem shots is often an interesting diversion. These could be short trap shots, high trap shots, shots from the rough, shots with a restricted backswing, low running shots to the green, and others. I have often practiced shots that I feared. This is a good method of developing confidence.

Occasionally, variety can be added by practicing with someone else. Stimulation can come from competing against a friend either in a putting contest or in tests of accuracy with other clubs.

One of the additional advantages that accrues from this type of practice is that you can obtain a fairly objective measure of your improvement or skill.

I have practiced competitive wedge shots against friends and found that a relative superiority in this field made it foolish for me to emphasize it in practice. It highlighted the fact that the reason my friend and I were equal in scoring was my relative deficiency in hitting greens with long irons, and his in hitting with short ones. I then practiced to pull level with him on the longer irons, slacking off on wedge practice, and the improvement was reflected in the scores.

On another occasion, a friend and I had a long putt contest. We each putted five balls, marking the pattern of shots. His pattern was so superior to mine that I adopted his method, with much more success.

On still another occasion, in a chipping contest, we used radically different methods but achieved the same good results. This kept both of us from investing time in experimenting with the other's method when it was probable that little would be gained.

Generally, however, it is not a good idea to plan to practice with others. It is hard enough to get one's own person to the practice tee. In addition, you may acquire the habit of wanting to practice with someone else. The difficulties that crop up in such an arrangement will cause a decline of interest. It is better to have the habit of enjoying solitary practice. Still and all, occasional joint practice adds variety and provides for a healthy exchange of information.

Experimentation of any kind is conducive to increasing interest. This experimentation can be done on the spur of the moment while on the practice tee. Experimentation can also be done in advance. If you develop certain ideas about a stroke, you can try them out in your mind first. Thinking about one's method of play can very easily eliminate mistakes before you get to the golf course. This has happened to me. For a long time I had difficulty controlling recovery shots when I had a very steep lie on the side of a bunker or trap near the green. My wedge shot would be unusually high, pulled to the left, and short. When I played this same shot from level ground I was generally close to the flag. One day I thought, "If I will be sure that my stance on a sidehill shot is as near as possible to my stance on level ground, the ball should chip out normally." I tried it, and it worked.

11th, SECRET

How to Avoid
Habits that Kill Interest

Unhappiness very often creeps up on us in insidious ways. Illness, fatigue, anxiety, and boredom can gradually erode our interest in life. Such things can also undermine a healthy interest in golf. In order to guard against these dangers, here are some sound precautions:

1. *Avoid playing or practicing when you do not feel well.* Undue physical fatigue leads to poor golfing habits in addition to conditioning you against practice. However, most fatigue is emotional in origin, and this type can be relieved by forced exercise and recreation.

2. *Avoid habits that are generally considered to lead to poor health levels.* If you can, avoid alcohol. If you cannot, restrict the drinking. Many talented golfers have been ruined as their social drinking degenerated into alcoholism. This is the saddest golf "secret" of them all.

3. *Always stop practicing while you are still interested.* If you practice until your interest fails, you will tend not to want to return.

4. *Practice first the shots that require the least effort.* Begin with the putter and work backwards to the woods. This insures that the great stroke-saving shots will get their due of attention. If you practice wood shots first you are apt to tire, and will have no interest for further short game practice.

5. *Do not complicate your swing.* Of two ways of hitting the ball that seem equally effective, it is better to adopt the swing that involves the fewest complications. In addition to the inherent value of simplifying the stroke, there is the advantage of being able to hit more shots with the same total amount of effort. There is also a natural tendency for the easier swing to be learned more quickly. It has been found that of two or more acts which precede a rewarding state of affairs, that act which involves the least expenditure of effort receives the greatest amount of net reinforcement.

6. *Do not play or practice under conditions that create anxiety or dislike.* There are so many such situations that it is not possible to list them all. Some that come to mind are: playing in uncomfortable weather, playing with uncongenial persons, playing with golfers who are either much better or much worse than you are, playing when there are more important things to be attended to, and betting more than you can afford to lose.

7. *Do not practice when you feel you are getting nowhere by practicing.* If you are in a golfing blind alley and you know from your records that considerable practice is not resulting in any considerable improvement, your interest will deteriorate very quickly. Under these circumstances, you must take lessons immediately before you develop an interest-killing frustration.

Generally, a condition of this kind is brought about by a misunderstanding of some golf principle. If, for instance, you have read that it is advisable to lead with the left wrist as Demaret does and you have misinterpreted the execution, you may be using a method ineffective for you merely because a great golfer has advocated it. This grows out of what is known as the "halo effect." It simply means we are apt to be overawed by authority. Sometimes this places us in blind alleys. It is at this point that we require some other authority to put us straight.

12th, **SECRET**

For Greater Pleasure

and Improvement, Keep Golf Records

I have derived golf enjoyment in many ways, but as I look back I find that the greatest pleasures have come from keeping, tabulating, and examining my golf scores and records. I have kept such records for more than 20 years. Here are some of the many benefits I have derived which have contributed to faster improvement:

1. *I know precisely what I am shooting now,* and how this compares with previous shooting, and I can see what improvement I can hope to make in the future.

2. Since I periodically strike averages, *every stroke is always important* to me no matter how poorly I may be playing any

given round. If I can eke out an 86 instead of an 87, this is just as important as getting 72 instead of 73 in a round that will have to be averaged in with nine other rounds. As a consequence, I have a very strong habit of being careful.

3. Since, in effect, my records force me into careful play, I have habitually played under a tension of my own making. *I am thus habituated to pressure* and do not feel that I am affected by it.

4. *My records provide me with a measuring stick for the effectiveness of practice.* My scores will reveal if any particular type of practice is paying off. In addition to round scores, I may also keep records of practice shots, just as a scientist does in his conduction of an experiment. These records help to keep me out of golfing blind alleys.

5. *My records prevent golfing confusion.* I do not underestimate or overestimate my golfing abilities merely because a few rounds are poor and a few are good. I know a genuine slump from a false one and do not abandon satisfactory methods of play for problematical new ones.

Without records I could not tell how my general game has stood up for the past ten years. For instance, this past year I scored the lowest average I ever had, but, except for the totaling of games, I would never have known it. I do not "feel" that I am playing one whit better than last year, five years ago, or ten years ago. Often I have the delusion that in a previous part of my personal golfing history I was driving or putting much better, but the records fail to show it.

6. *My records enable me to maintain a golfing equanimity,* deriving a long-pull satisfaction from the game. I am not disturbed by events that do not justify disturbance.

7. *There is a keen pleasure in posting scores, striking averages and noticing trends.* This pleasure is superimposed on the pleasure derived from the golf itself.

8. *Learning is more rapid if one keeps records.* It has been found that students who are continuously aware of the standings of their daily and weekly grades perform better than those who are not so informed.

9. *By keeping records, I have provided myself with a permanent golfing partner—myself.* This makes golf so interesting that even solitary play is stimulating. I have played many more rounds by myself than I have with others, and they have provided a unique and pleasurable form of recreation.

13th, SECRET

How to

Keep and Use Golf Records

The most important records I keep are the golf scores. They are kept chronologically by months. An average is struck at the end of each ten rounds, twenty rounds, forty rounds, and at the end of the year. Here is the record for my play in 1958 on the par 72 Augusta Country Club course.

There were a number of questions I was able to answer through an examination of these scores.

1958

	Jan.	Feb. March	April	May	June	July	Aug.	Aug.	Sept.	Oct.	Oct.	Nov.	Dec.
1	82	80	81	78		77	78	78	75	76	75	76	
2	76	88	82	84		77	80	77	78	79	76	74	
3	76	82	78	81		83	82	78	78	77	78	76	
4	76	81	77	84	No	79	75	80	77	78	78	73	No
5	74	78	80	80		81	79	74	78	77	76	72	
6	76	83	78	77	Play	79	78	80	78	76	77	77	Play
7	84	86	81	74		80	77	82	76	77	74	77	
8	79	83	78	76		79	79	80	77	77	75	80	
9	79	80	83	77		80	74	82	75	78	77	76	
10	78	81	79	79		76	75	82	75	77	76	75	
10 Rounds	78.0	82.2	79.7	79.0		79.1	77.7	79.3	76.3	77.2	76.2	75.6	
20 Rounds	80.1		79.4			78.4		77.8		76.7			
40 Rounds	79.8					78.1				76.7			
Yearly Average 110 Rounds	78.2												

1. *Was there any improvement?* Since the 1957 average was 77.3 and the 1958 average was 78.2, it appeared that, in spite of practice, my game had deteriorated. However, I noted that in 1957 I had not played in the winter months. Yet, after I eliminated these four months from comparison, I still showed an apparent loss of skill.

Finally, I saw a ray of hope. When I compared my 1957 scores in September and October with the same months in 1958, I found that my latter scores were almost a stroke better, with an average of 76.6 compared with the previous September and October average of 77.4. It was possible that I had improved a stroke instead of deteriorating that much. This was later verified by 1959 scores which dropped to a record low.

Although I do not consider myself a person who is easily discouraged, I could have become so except for what the analysis of the records showed. I can think of no greater golfing tragedy than an unjustified discouragement that ruins one's game at the very moment when the actual prospects are most hopeful.

2. *How widely do my scores fluctuate?* It looked as if single scores could not give me much information. In a series of 10 rounds, there could be a fluctuation of 4 to 10 strokes between my highest and lowest scores. Over the route of a whole year, I varied from a low of 72 to a high of 88—16 strokes.

3. *How significant are 10-round averages?* Apparently they are quite unreliable. The lowest 10-round average was 75.6. The highest was 82.2. These averages by themselves do not mean too much. They become significant only when they are correlated with other factors, such as weather conditions.

4. *How many scores does it take to indicate real changes?* Well, we have seen that even a yearly average can be misleading at first glance. However, records show that 20 rounds of golf seem to be enough to give a fair picture of what is going on.

We note that in 1958, 20-round averages reflected the effect of the winter months. There followed a steady "improvement," with best scores showing up in late summer and early fall. Of course, these reveal "improvements" which merely reflect better course conditions. They do not necessarily indicate improvement unless the same months are compared with those of the previous year.

Many other analyses of the above records are possible, and there are also other types of records which are useful. I sometimes keep separate records of the results of practice if I am working on a particular weakness. If my records do not show any improvement, I do not expect any when I play. If the records show that the weakness is being corrected, I play better —both because I *am* better and because my records have removed anxiety.

5. *How much improvement can I expect?* It has been said that golf is a "humbling game." Thousands of great athletes have fallen by the wayside in trying to master it. Even larger numbers of men eminently successful in the business and professional world have been casualties. On one occasion, I witnessed a determined club member at the Shackmaxon Club in New Jersey hit numberless balls into the lake at the old 17th hole. When he ran out of balls, he threw in his clubs and bag, and would have thrown in the caddy if he hadn't eluded him. One of our Augusta club members, Jake Howard, Sr., completed the grand slam of balls, clubs, bag and *caddy* at the famous Sea Island golf course, thus adding considerably to our enjoyment of the game.

If one keeps records, the "humbling" aspect of golf can be removed. It has made me realistic as to how much improvement I can expect from any given amount of practice or play, and it has given me a healthy respect for scores that to others might seem high. Too much significance is given to the scores of leaders in golf tournaments and not enough to the true average of professionals as a group. I have only casually examined the average scores during the Masters, but I hazard they must be about 78 or so. In any case, many are unrealistic about how much one should or can improve. This unrealism is cured when you keep records. An average improvement of one stroke a year is healthy progress.

14th, SECRET

The Key to Accuracy

The greatest single principle to apply in the development of accuracy is to *eliminate variables*. It is the most important single rule for experimentation within the broad framework of the known fundamentals, and it can lead to the discovery of important techniques. This is the only way in which the so-called "repeating swing" can be achieved. The secret is so important that with it, it is possible for a novice golfer to take charge of his own instruction after he has learned the simple fundamentals of grip, stance, and swing.

To understand what we mean by "eliminate the variables," let us imagine that there exists a mechanical golfer built like a human. However, when we start the motor, we note the operation of the robot is very erratic, so we decide to tighten the machine up at the points that seem logical.

First, we see that the top of the mechanical man sways a good bit, so we bolt the head to the ceiling in such a way that it does not move. We have eliminated one variable. (The head is still.)

Second, we see that the guiding lever arm has a loose joint in the middle, so we tighten this section so it does not bend. (We now have a straight left arm.)

Third, we note the lower part of the machine dances about the floor, so we eliminate this variable by tightening up the bolts that hold it to the floor. (Controlled foot action.)

Fourth, we find that the club twists as it strikes the ball. We eliminate this variable by seeing that the robot's hands and the shaft are firmly welded together. (Improved grip.)

We continue doing this for every variable we can find, until accuracy can no longer be improved upon. Of course, we make some concessions. Sometimes we find we can have a permissible error in accuracy in order to develop additional power, but this will occur in the relatively few distance shots.

The principle of eliminating variables will serve as a guide to instruction when the experts disagree. For instance, a good playing professional recently advocated re-gripping the club at the top of the backswing. This introduces a variable. Again, on principle, it is risky to habitually slice or hook shots. By so doing we are introducing variables. Some years ago, one of the finest putters in Georgia cut all his putts. This introduces a variable. He would have been better without it. Further, there is some disagreement among professionals as to the proper action of the left foot. Is it better to roll it, or to lift the heel off the ground? According to our theory, a variable would be eliminated if the foot is rolled rather than lifted. Hence if you are strong enough to obtain satisfactory power, it would be best to eliminate the variable of lifting the heel.

Another application of the principle: If you are faced with a problem shot, use the method which has fewer variables. For

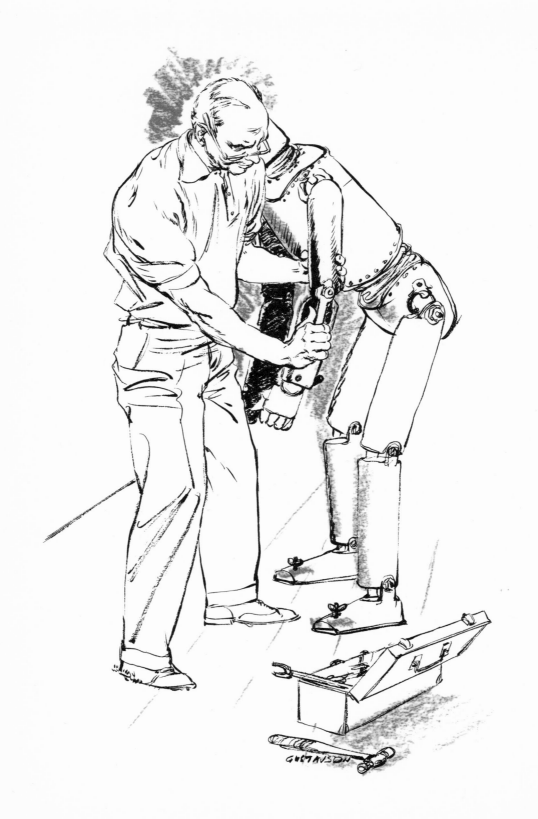

instance: there are two ways of playing a cross-wind. One is "always play into the wind," which would mean that such shots would have to be hooked or faded. The other is "use your normal swing, but allow for the wind." The first method involves the addition of two variables—the wind and the degree of hook or fade to be imparted. The second involves only one variable—the wind. The second method has the probability of greater success.

Other illustrations of eliminating variables follow.

You have finally learned to hit a straight shot with the woods and you now wish to be able to slice when necessary. You have a choice of three methods of slicing.

1. Open the stance.
2. Open the blade.
3. Cut the ball by hitting outside in.

The second method seems to involve the addition of the smallest number of variables. Only the position of the club in the hands is changed. No muscular changes are required. In the other two methods, considerable muscular re-orientation is demanded.

Eminent golfing authorities are in disagreement on how to control distance in blasting out of traps. Some advise regulating distance by taking more or less sand. Others advise using the same stroke but varying the power. Of the two, the latter seems to involve the addition of fewer variables and is theoretically sounder.

The wind is in your face on a par three. You have the ability to play a choked four iron, a medium five iron, or a full six iron. You feel confident with all three clubs. If we follow our plan of eliminating variables, we will play the five iron. This is not too doubtful a case, as I believe most good golfers would play the hole in this fashion, but there are many golfing situations, from putts to drives, in which the decision is not quite so clear.

We can see from the above examples that the use of matched sets of clubs is of distinct advantage to the modern golfer, since they have removed many muscular variables which old-timers had to bring to bear to achieve long shots, medium shots, and short shots with one club. The sand wedge has removed some variables in trap shots. The steel shaft has eliminated the ever-changing variable of the "whip" and "torque" of the wood shaft. The all-weather grip removed another variable, and the elimination of the stymie removed an interesting variable that should have been retained.

There are many kinds of variables. There are the mechanical ones we have indicated above. There are also times when rain, wind, or the lay of the land introduces variables. There are even psychological variables. In all cases, performance is more accurate to the extent that variables are eliminated. If this rule is successfully applied, improvement is automatic.

15th, SECRET

The Meaning of "Golf Bugs"

The basic fundamentals of golf are well known and provide no problems to beginners. Yet, within the framework of these principles, there is enough variation of form among topnotch golfers to confuse us. If we become tempted to model ourselves first after one player and then another, we are headed for disaster. The inherent trouble lies in the "golf bugs."

Many golfers of equal ability have easily recognizable differences of form. For each of these different forms, there are adjustments and modifications that must be made. We call these modifications "golf bugs" and no swing is without them.

You see then the danger of modeling ourselves after more than one person. The over-all swing may be fine, but we have to be shown or find out for ourselves what these new "bugs" are. ("Bugs" are also apparent to a degree in different sets of clubs, particularly with putters.)

Hogan is an advocate of placing the ball close to the line of the left heel. This is done for both woods and irons. Such placement is good according to our theory, since it eliminates the variable of changing the position of the ball with each club used. However, in order for Hogan to hit shots with accuracy he has had to develop a compensating variable by changing the position of his right foot.

On the other hand, Peter Thomson has demonstrated that he can regulate distance and maintain accuracy by shifting the position of the ball. In order to do this, he has had to work out a number of modifications which in turn compensate for "bugs" inherent in his method.

Perhaps the matter of the "bugs" can be highlighted by reference to the radically different methods of Jimmy Nichols, the former one-armed world champion golfer, and Ed Furgol, former open champion. Both play par golf, but the similarity virtually ends at that point. Nichols lost his right arm in an auto accident many years ago. He was already a very good golfer. He tried desperately to play left-handed and failed miserably. One day, while practicing, he gave up in disgust, but as he left the fairway, he drew back his two iron and took a back-handed swipe at the ball. To his amazement it took off in a perfect trajectory over the caddy's head. He had used a "right-handed" swing with his left. (Incidentally, we might point out that in effect he had removed at one swipe all the variables he had added when he was using the unfamiliar left-handed swing.) Nichols had to make a number of modifications in stance and grip in order to perfect his swing and bring his scores back to the low 70's. He had to find out for himself what the "bugs" were. This led to modifications of stance and grip that are not orthodox at all.

A similar condition exists with Ed Furgol. In his case, it was his left arm that was rendered almost useless. With all due respect to a courageous golfer, his swing contains contorted action incompatible with the orthodox idea of how to make a club meet a ball. He, too, had to discover the "bugs" in his particular manner of hitting a golf shot.

This is true for all styles of play. There is danger in modeling oneself after more than one player. It was Bobby Jones' great fortune that he modeled himself after Stewart Maiden, with his famous Carnoustie swing. It is said that, at a distance, the form of the two players looked identical. Jones was able not only to capitalize on the learning and experience of his teacher, but also had a ready source of information about "bugs" peculiar to that swing and how to correct them.

Some methods of play have more "bugs" than others. In such cases a swing may have to be rebuilt from the ground up, or the golfer will play in a blind alley. Therefore, as many good teaching professionals know, if you already have a heavy investment of time in a swing, it is more efficient to stick by it, working the "bugs" out one by one.

One of my golfing friends changed from a fair putter to an excellent one when he abandoned a number of compensatory adjustments and simply eliminated two variables. His problem for some time had been that of direction. Ostensibly there was nothing wrong with his putting stroke. He had adopted the form of a golf professional who was quite good and had had considerable instruction from him. Something minute was apparently occuring during the process of the stroke, a random variation that caused some putts to go to the right of the hole and some to the left. I suggested that he set up an experimental putting situation on a carpet. After a number of sterile putting sessions in which there seemed to be no consistent pattern, he noticed that, on occasion, when he appeared to "get in the groove," he would make a very nice run of putts. Suddenly he had a flash of insight. He realized that after those occasions when the putting device did not return the ball properly and he had to retrieve it himself, he would generally miss. He concluded that his trouble lay in a change of stance or grip or both. He became considerably more accurate by simply marking his feet positions on the carpet and his thumb position on the grip during a "good run."

16th, SECRET

Handle Compensatory

Adjustments with Care

In trying to overcome an error, a person is apt to accept whatever remedy produces the quickest good results. This often means another error to compensate for the first. As an illustration, a golfer who is slicing will often change his grip by putting his right hand further under the club. But it may be that the slicing is caused by the stance or hip action. He now has two faults instead of one, though he may well correct his slice, and he has made it more difficult to hold on to his game, since there is a probable mathematical limit of improvement for each form and for each combined group of "compensatory" adjustments. Also, with such a compensatory adjustment, what is gained in direction is lost perhaps in power or touch—an additional weakness for which some other compensatory adjustment must be worked out, which in turn breeds other weaknesses.

The answer is that compensatory adjustments should be made within the orthodox limits unless there is a physical handicap. A grip or swing that you are accustomed to can stand slight changes only. Greater changes involve too much relearning. To prevent extreme compensatory adjustments, get outside help.

If the error is comparatively minor, a good way to make the correction is to do so gradually to prevent overcompensation; otherwise a slice may turn into an equally disastrous hook.

One method of avoiding the dangers of compensatory maladjustments is to search for ways to eliminate variables. Let us suppose that one is missing chip shots because he occasionally hits one too "fat" or "tops." A compensatory adjustment might be to abandon the shot altogether and roll the ball up with a putter. Since this solution adds the variable of the terrain it is not a good answer. A much better solution would be one that permanently eliminated some variable. In all likelihood, this could be achieved by resting the right elbow upon the hip for greater reliability.

When an adjustment in grip, for instance, exceeds the orthodox limits, it is a good sign that there is a gross error in form in some other feature of the swing. This should be an indication that one should return to his original grip and search elsewhere for the cause of the trouble. The simplest way to conduct this search is to run through the usual check-points.

The danger of compensatory adjustments is that they not only

relapses because of the addition of variables. (Other phases of this problem will be dealt with later under "Don't Practice Strengths.")

17 th. **SECRET**

Why Golf Lessons Fail

Often a person with a golfing flaw will consult his pro and is straightened out. Later, when he tries his new stroke on the course, it doesn't seem to work. There are a number of reasons why golf lessons fail.

1. *The player is concentrating so hard on the new form that he neglects to do the usual golf thinking* that has to accompany the stroke. For instance, he may not consider the usual factors of the condition of the green, the putting problem, the distance to the green, or golf management. The answer to this is that the new golf stroke should be practiced until it has been "over-learned." When this has come about, the mind will not be si-phoned away from problems of over-all thinking. In the mean-time, if you recognize the danger, it is possible to finesse the

problem by attacking it serially. First work out the decisions of management, then tackle the execution of the shot.

2. *The form is correct, but he has not learned the idiosyncracies of that particular stroke.* It may be that his ball rolls further or stops more quickly than before. He must acquire a new scale of touch. Incidentally, this is one phase of golf that has not received much treatment in instruction. The present attitude is that this is simply a matter of muscle memory, and learners are left to their own devices. In putting, chipping, trap shots, and approaches, "touch" is of the essence in golf. Since this touch varies with different methods of hitting shots, it should be practiced. And, since it is seldom that two shots are of the same length, golf practice without constant change in the length of the shot is inefficient. Such practice violates our rule that practice should duplicate playing conditions.

3. *Poor luck is operating.* He may be stroking better but scoring worse. He needs to average more scores.

4. *He has waited too long to try the stroke on the course, and has forgotten some of the instruction.*

5. *He tried the stroke without first warming up.* When he learned the new form, he no doubt hit many shots. When he went on the course, the advantage of the warm-up was missing.

6. *There was a loss of confidence when applying the shot.* It would have been different if the pro had been along to give him assurance.

7. *Something has occurred to create confusion in the golfer.* Confusion generally comes about when instruction has not been completely absorbed, when some bit of instruction has emotional overtones, and particularly if a decision is hanging fire. The longer the indecision, the more confusion (and anxiety) is generated.

8. *The golfer does not realize the vast number of shots re-*

quired to put into effect a new method that a professional can teach in five minutes. Even Hogan would practice for months using a minor improvement in grip before he would dare try this change in important play.

9. *While the golfer was under the professional's tutelage, small mistakes were corrected continuously, but now the golfer tends to stray from the instructional beam.* The learner should keep returning to the professional for further instruction as fast as he relapses, until all the remedial instruction has become part of the over-all pattern of the stroke.

There is also the problem of the "groove." Remember my golfing friend who, when correcting his putting, occasionally made many consecutive good shots when his golfing environment was standardized. The same thing often occurs during a practice session. After hitting a number of balls toward a caddy, the problem of aiming disappears. The stance has only slight modifications. Often our feet sink slightly into the ground. The pro directly modifies other features of our swing. Altogether there is some apparent improvement which will not necessarily transfer to the course. One of our practice fairways has a slope, so that, in taking stances, the feet are slightly higher than the position of the ball. Learn to hit a straight drive on this fairway and it becomes a hook when you play from level tees.

10. *The golfer has been fooled by "feel."* If a person has developed a slice, for instance, his pro corrects it by advising him to hit inside out. When he first begins to make the correction, the new stroke "feels funny." It seems exaggerated and unnatural, but since the shot finally comes off well, he accepts the method. The new stroke feels less and less awkward as time goes on, until it seems perfectly natural.

This is the danger point. He is so accustomed to the need for the "feel" of swinging inside out that he tries to recapture this sensation by further accentuating the inside-out arc. Lo and behold, an in-out feel that once changed a slice into a straight ball is turning the straight ball into a ducking hook. Similar overcompensation occurs in putting. Beware of being tricked by a "feel" after the shot is grooved.

11. *The new stroke is working well, but some other department of his game may be off,* or the improvement may not reveal itself in scores except over a longer period of time.

18th, SECRET

What to Do

about Idiosyncracies

One of the minor vices of some golfers is to believe that an idiosyncracy (a deviation from orthodox form) of a good player is a major element of a successful stroke or swing. Some idiosyncracies are really minor adjustments to a flaw in the swing, and are only necessary for a given golfer. Some idiosyncracies develop because the owner "falsely" believes that they are essential; by giving him confidence, these then become "genuinely" essential.

Many idiosyncracies in older golfers date back to mannerisms picked up as youngsters, and have no meaning except that they are long-time habits without which they would feel uncomfortable. Some such habits border on the superstitious. I know one

golfer who, when he was 17, won a tight match from a better player. It happened that he had a full bladder at the time. The further the round progressed, the more tension developed in his bladder and the better he played. To this day he will not relieve himself during an important match.

Some idiosyncracies develop out of emotional involvement. A golfing friend of mine used to aim as much as 30 degrees to the right of his target. A person whom he disliked had been the first to tell him of his error. He therefore denied that there was anything wrong with his stance, and then got into the habit of defending it. When this player heard that Hogan played with his right foot back, he stated, "I actually anticipated Hogan's theories." When I questioned him about it, he seemed to get excited. Suspecting an emotional problem, I took a picture of his swing with a Polaroid camera. When he saw himself, he agreed to take a lesson.

Another acquaintance has had the fortunate experience of a long friendship with a great golfer. He goes through a preliminary ritual in taking his stance and making his waggle, which is calculating, quite deliberate and impressive. As his backswing begins, however, there is a contrasting frenzy of uncoordinated motion directed at a ball that, like a surprised quail, heads for the nearest cover. Here again we have an emotional involvement—and one I haven't the courage or the heartlessness to attempt to enucleate. What could or should I say if he, with dignity, should say, "That's how *Byron* advised me to swing!"?

Psychologically, the trouble in both of the above instances was that the players had acquired an emotionally vested interest in supporting an incorrect position—a common cause of error among intelligent golfers.

Idiosyncracies in poor players do no damage to others, but when they belong to one who plays well, it is apt to confuse his imitators into believing that the peculiarity (or the shadow) is the chief reason for his playing well, whereas it might be excessive practice (the substance) which has produced a noticeable skill.

We had an example of this in the realm of billiards. Willie Hoppe deviated from standard form. Instead of sighting from directly behind the ball, with the cue close to his side, he stroked the ball with the cue held away from his body. This was considered quite an unusual idiosyncracy. Hoppe learned to play when he was a child. In order to reach shots otherwise unplayable to him, he had to stretch his arms away from his body. After years of play, this became a part of his form, and he was playing too well to begin over.

Although it is possible that his unorthodox form contributed to his success, it is safer to assume that he had such great talent that he was able to carry a burden that would have handicapped those with less ability.

We are now posed with a problem. How can we distinguish between unorthodox form as such, and unorthodox form which may be equally as good as the standard methods or may even constitute our personal discovery? In my experience, *the characteristic of a basic improvement in method has been dramatic and sudden improvement in the behavior of the ball.* When this occurs, the chances are that something useful has indeed been discovered and should be tested well. Generally speaking, such attempts at discoveries should only be tried by those who are already completely saturated with an orthodox knowledge of the game or a particular shot.

19th SECRET

How to
Make Faith Work for You

Success in anything is hardly possible without faith, and this is true of success in golf. One way to develop golfing faith is to study experts.

Such watching builds up confidence that difficult shots can be made and that normal shots *should* be made. This causes many golfers to improve spontaneously, simply from the psychological lift that comes from a change in his attitude towards what *can* be done. Sometimes the improvement is permanent.

For instance, in track and field events, as soon as a given record is surpassed, there are almost immediate further breakings of what *was* the old record.

It was very difficult to jump over 6 feet, to run a mile in less than four minutes, and to pole-vault over 15 feet. But as soon as it was first done, there was a rash of athletes surpassing the old marks.

An appropriate story is told about Ralph Guldahl's small nephew. He was in a bicycle shop with his parents when he spotted a tricycle similar to his own at home. He rode it around

the store several times, then promptly fell off when his brother yelled out to him, "It's only got two wheels!" It was really a bicycle, and he did not learn to ride a bicycle until some years later.

An obvious cause of low modern scores is the improvement in equipment, but an equally important cause has been the persisting psychological effect of the achievements of great golfers. Golf became a much easier game the moment Walter Travis displayed his genius with a putter; when Vardon showed what accuracy was possible with the woods; when Hagen revealed the possibilities of recovery shots; when Jones consistently began dipping into the sixties; when Hogan demonstrated what could be done with dedicated practice; and when Sarazen recently demonstrated at St. Andrews what could be done by a senior golfer.

We hear much about the need for being realistic and, in truth, it is an important principle in solving problems. But golf, like life, is difficult to handle if we rely too much upon hard and fast rules. We seem to drift from reality when we speak of an intangible like faith. Yet golf is a projection of life, and there are times in life when it is better to be realistically unrealistic. It is best for the individual golfer to believe that there is no limit to what he can do, for it is by such beliefs that he can continuously surpass himself.

It is also best for the game of golf if all of us have faith that we can excel, though obviously everyone cannot be tops in a competitive game. The stimulus of this faith acting upon millions of golfers will help raise the level of present play. In the raising of this level, we shall experience the pleasure that comes when we share in the excitement of witnessing original methods break through physical and psychological barriers to new records.

If a golfer cannot believe that he can be *best*, he must believe that he can be *better*. Even such a limited faith can lead him step by step to a brand of golf he might never have believed possible.

20th SECRET

No Transfer of Training

In previous generations, it was believed that the mind that was trained in one field would automatically be better fitted to do other things also. For instance, it was thought that training in mathematics would help you with Greek, that a good billiard player would automatically be an excellent putter, and that a polo player would have no difficulty in learning such a similar game as golf. Unfortunately, this is not true. Many experiments have shown that each new type of learning is almost always different from all other types. When there is some similarity, a portion of what one learns in one skill or game will carry on to the next, but this is not usual.

Willie Hoppe, the billiard champion, was astonished that he could not putt. Pete Bostwick, the great polo player, plays creditably, but he is not in the same class with himself as a polo player. Babe Didricksen had a natural talent for all sports but, in order to become good in golf, she had to become almost as hard a practicer as Ben Hogan.

I have participated in most of the sports and games popular

today and do not recall any instance in which what I had learned in one field was of noticeable value in another. For instance, chess can be quite a difficult and complicated game. I have had the good fortune to play against nationally known players and, occasionally, have defeated them, but almost any good country player can defeat me at the more simple game of checkers. I have a close friend who plays both chess and checkers. I defeat him in the one game; he defeats me easily in the other. It is not a question of talent. I worked diligently at learning chess but only dabbled with checkers. With him, conditions were reversed.

There is one kind of learning in which substantial "transfer" can occur. This is the field of attitudes and principles. If I had attacked the problem of learning checkers with the same attitude I had toward chess, and if I had applied basic psychological principles to the process of learning, the results would have been approximately the same.

All this comes under the general rule of "no transfer of training," which when understood will help us avoid wasting time by practicing something which will not be of golfing benefit. In this connection, it is likely that there are few, if any, exercises that will materially assist the golfer.

The practical application of this means that practice will not be efficient unless we *practice the very thing we wish to learn, and unless we practice it under circumstances that duplicate precisely all conceivable factors that apply to the golfing problem.* We see, as developing from this principle, that medal and match play, winter and summer play, friendly and competitive golf, windy weather and calm weather, flat or hilly courses, and indoor play all present changes in the golfing situation which the golfer has to learn as new skills.

If we are thinking of individual shots, we see then that the ideal would be to practice a shot at the very point on the course and almost at the same time that it was missed. This is not practical, but he who is most careful in seeing that his practice shots duplicate his playing shots will learn the game most quickly.

A Tip

on How to Remember

Shots are often missed because of an attempt on the part of the golfer to concentrate on two or more things simultaneously. This produces confusion. It is much easier if we remember things serially. On an important shot, for instance, the "count-down" might be: ball at left heel, feet firmly planted, firm left hand, right elbow close in, head still, straight left arm, and finally, firm hit!

If such a series or a similar one is run through until it is automatic, good form will be easily remembered. If a fault develops, whatever remedy is suggested by the pro can be incorporated in the series. Eventually the only thing to try to remember is your final improvement.

It is a good idea to use words or labels to help you recall how to hit certain shots. I once had a great deal of trouble with a trap shot when I was close to the bank. I noted the ease with

which Snead made this in a Master's tournament. I copied his form and I can recall this form by simply saying to myself, "This requires the Snead shot." By recalling "Hogan's chip", I also automatically adopt a reasonable fascimile of the Hogan method of chipping. I find that in the areas in which I thus verbalize I have the least difficulty in remembering how the shot is to be played.

This makes use of the Gestalt principle in psychology, which, in general, means that we tend to learn by wholes rather than by parts. It would be very difficult for a caddy to analyze piece-meal the swing of any particular club member, but he can often mimic the swing in its entirety if he recalls the total image. In this connection, Bobby Jones states that there is too much con-cern with the niceties of the mechanics of the game and not enough emphasis on just hitting the ball with the club.

Perhaps a compromise is in order. Learning in the early stages can be broken up by verbalizing serially—the countdown —until it becomes automatic. Then concentrate only on the last thing learned. The latter will not only assist you to incorporate an improvement in your swing, but will also prevent you from thinking of those parts of your swing with which the conscious mind should not be concerned.

22nd, **SECRET**

Understanding

"Trial and Error"

There are certain broad principles of golf which are useful in the rapid development of a sound swing. Such principles have been ably expounded by Bobby Jones, Tommy Armour, Percy Boomer, Ben Hogan and others. I once witnessed how quickly they can be taught. Beginning with a 34-year-old woman who had never swung a club, Harvey Penick set up for her a mechanical pattern which in thirty minutes produced a very good-looking golf swing resulting in many good shots. She began to play almost daily and in three months shot a 39 for nine holes from men's tees.

However, the fine tuning of golf can take a lifetime and is mostly trial and error.

Thorndike and others discovered that cats, dogs, chicks, monkeys and other animals, when attacking a new problem, first tried a number of hit and miss solutions. Those things which failed they gradually abandoned. Those which led to success were "stamped in" and retained. What this emphasized was that a successful performance is not necessarily the result of conscious thought, but is rather caused by associations produced by subconscious mechanisms of the body. It is significant that when Snead was asked how he did it, he said that he really did not know. Hogan, on the other hand, has been credited with being able to take his swing apart and put it back together again. This is to some extent true on a broad scale, but how each muscle learns its duties no one knows specifically.

We must assume that this trial and error process is gone through by an infinite number of our bodily mechanisms and hence can only come about by much previous trial and error. Gross skills come first, then skills within the correct gross skills, and then skills within *these* skills, until we come to the fine tuning required for a long side hill putt, breaking to the right on a fast green.

Trial and error learning is most important in learning the short game. So much attention has been focussed on proper form in full shots that we tend to forget the extreme importance of being able to hit the ball varying distances in approaches, trap shots, chips and putts. The inability to gauge these distances accounts for the loss of most of our strokes. In this department of golf form seems relatively unimportant, and trial and error learning all-important. Hogan's recent difficulties around the greens has hardly come about because of any deterioration in gross form. There has simply been some muscular forgetting where distance is concerned, and considerable trial and error relearning is the remedy.

The three necessary elements, then for efficient learning in golf are the mechanical fundamentals, the application of psychology, and considerable trial and error learning. The latter requires time.

23rd, SECRET

Using Attention
to Speed Learning

It has been found that to speed learning it is vital to practice and play with *attention*. Practice by itself is not enough. If a golf professional has two students of equal ability, the attentive one will develop into a better golfer.

Lackadaisical practice is very inefficient, and can be harmful. If you practice carelessly, an attitude of carelessness may be transferred to actual play. Then, too, unnecessary or incorrect movements may find their way into the swing and, almost without our being aware of it, we have added destructive variables.

You may ask, "But how do I become attentive? Can I make myself pay attention to what I'm doing even though my mind tends to wander?" You can in ways that *make use of the principle of tension*.

If you think for a moment, you will recall that the eyes of a person who is very anxious to learn—say a flier being briefed on the target of the day and knowing that his life may depend on how well he learns—are under strain; he leans forward in his chair; the muscles in his jaws and other parts of the body tighten. He is under both mental and physical tension. The right kind of tension produces concentration, just as concentration

produces tension. A smile can produce better feelings merely by association.

Another method which inspires attention is to *set up an artificial competitive situation.* This competition can be against others or directed against yourself by making a game out of solitary play or practice. By such means, it is possible to develop the habit of carefulness so that you can go for years without hitting a careless shot.

An incidental but highly important result of setting up artificial forms of competition is that it will tend to immunize you against pressure. At one time I coached a high school basketball team. I realized that many games were decided by slim margins —very often by the opposition's relative ability to make foul shots. I had my players practice such shots at great length and, as a result, we had a nice competitive advantage. However, when the game was very close, players who could shoot well in practice would fail miserably. I then changed the practice sessions so that each day the boys would compete by attempting to break their own record for successive shots. As they approached their previous records, tension was quite apparent and they were forced to learn how to handle it. In both basketball and golf situations where I created artificial tension, I found the best antidote was attention combined with a muscular relaxation that prevented the activation of muscles unnecessary to the stroke, an activation known to golfers as "tightening up." This matter of "taking off the pressure" is treated more fully in a later chapter.

One of the good results of being perennially careful is that eventually you can combine this with being relaxed. If you are always careful, the habit of carefulness becomes a part of you, requiring no effort when a crisis comes along. On the other hand, carelessness breeds carelessness.

As William James [2] points out:

"The drunken Rip Van Winkle, in Jefferson's play, excuses

[2] James, William: *Psychology,* page 150, World Publishing Company, Cleveland, Ohio.

himself for every fresh dereliction by saying, 'I won't count this time!' Well! he may not count it, and a kind Heaven may not count it; but it is being counted none the less. Down among his nerve cells and fibres the molecules are counting it, registering and storing it up to be used against him when the next temptation comes."

So it is with the careless golf shot.

24th, **SECRET**

How to

Practice Remedial Golf

In order for a golfer to improve efficiently, practice must be remedial; that is it must eliminate the specific errors which are costing him the most strokes.

To do this, a number of steps are required:

1. He must have a system of locating errors.

2. He must periodically analyze these errors to see which are costing him the most strokes.

3. He must arrange his remedial practice (the correcting of these errors) so that he is devoting most of his practice time to the shots which are so costly.

4. He must be sure that he duplicates the exact shot which is causing him the greatest difficulty. (The best place is on the course itself, whenever possible.)

5. He must attempt to over-learn in the area in which he is weakest. This means that he must not only correct the error but must over-practice. Over-practice or over-learning is necessary to take care of forgetting. He must develop more skill than is actually necessary in play, because something is always forgotten.

6. He must try new techniques under playing conditions and, if they do not work, he must return to the practice grounds. He must again be sure that his practicing duplicates exactly the shot which is required, or the new skill will not show up in better performance.

The chief result of such remedial practice is that it saves the most strokes for the time invested. For instance, it is well known that after a layoff, the short game shows the most rapid deterioration. In returning to play after such an interval, you will be able to play much closer to your average if you practice putting, chipping and short approaches rather than the full shots.

In addition, remedial practice produces a very steady brand of golf. The amount of time devoted will determine the level of play, but at any level, it will produce scores that hover close to one's average. When one uses the remedial practice system, a poor performance in one category, such as in the irons, is compensated for in another category, such as putting, so that good luck and bad luck tend to cancel each other out. With remedial practice, there comes the day when all cylinders are operating well, and this produces some very satisfying scores.

Be realistic about your chances of improvement. If you do not engage in remedial practice, you cannot improve. To paraphrase Newton, "An error put in motion will continue to be an error until acted upon by remedial practice." No error will disappear of its own accord. A golfer is not entitled to swear about a missed golf shot if he has missed this same shot previously and did not correct it in the meantime.

25th, **SECRET**

Don't Practice Strengths

There are a number of errors of practice which lead to inefficiency. A common one occurs when a golfer practices the very shot with which he has the greatest skill.

How could such an apparently obvious mistake be prevalent? Here are a few reasons:

1. *Because a golfer can make a given shot, he derives more pleasure from practicing it than a shot which continually causes him anguish.*

2. *He may not have the courage to make a public display of his weak shots.*

3. *The good shot he is practicing may have been a weak shot at one time, and he has allowed a good idea to become a somewhat unreasonable fixed idea through simple habit.*

4. *Poor form can force a golfer to practice strengths excessively and incorrectly.* It is possible for a person to get good results by excessive practice of a weak technique. I saw an example of this by a player who was very successful in using lofted clubs close to the green, when a less lofted club was indicated. Although he did very well with his shot, he attained this by excessive practice which could have been better apportioned to his putting, which was only fair.

Practice alone is insufficient. It is inextricably tied to form. If the form is poor, practice will hopelessly fixate that form. Each form has its upper limits beyond which practice runs into a disproportionately low improvement for a given amount of time.

It is vital, therefore, that the golfer undertake a ceaseless quest for good form, and get it as early in his instruction as he can.

5. *He may make the error of not understanding the law of diminishing returns.* This simply means that it can be dangerous to try to become "too good" with any given club. There comes a point in every shot at which additional practice does not produce an equivalent improvement in the score.

A concrete example of the application of this is the following: The problem to be solved is that when you are off the green you are taking three and four to get down instead of two. There are several solutions. With the *first,* you can practice putting until you learn to get down in one. With the *second,* you can practice chipping until you are so accurate that it always leaves a "gimme." The *third,* which is the most efficient, would be to practice chipping and putting together until you could reasonably be expected to go down in two. The first two "solutions" would require excessive practice.

Billy Casper and Paul Runyan are two examples of golfers who have drawn big dividends from a selective investment of practice time by concentrating on their short game. However, this does not mean that the short game should be practiced *ad infinitum*. After a good short game has been stabilized, an analysis of your play may well show diminishing returns from such practice, and the time will then have come to attack other weaknesses that are revealed to be more costly.

6. Still another common error, which we have indicated previously by implication, is that *a person is not practicing his true weakness.* He may be practicing what is only apparently a weakness. To establish the weakness with the first priority on his time, it is necessary for him to analyze his records.

26th, **SECRET**

When Practice

Does Not Make Perfect

There are times when practice does not show up in lower scores. When this is true, the following causes should be considered:

1. *You are practicing shots for which there is little demand on your course.* Years ago, I played on several courses which de-

manded a good drive followed by medium and short irons. If I had practiced with a two iron, it would not have shown up in the scores. Concentrate on practicing shots for which there is much demand on your course. Where most of the holes are from 325 to 370 yards, there is a big demand for comparatively short irons and birdie-length putts. If you are practicing woods, long irons, trap shots, and long putts, there can be only a limited improvement in scoring.

Of course, there is some danger in practicing only those shots which your home course demands. You will find that if you switch your playing to a shorter, longer, or narrower course than you are used to, your scores will rise. During the war, Cary Middlecoff was stationed at Fort Gordon in my home town of Augusta. The army had taken over the old Forest Hills golf course, and Cary had many opportunities to play. The course is comparatively short and requires accurate rather than long tee shots. Middlecoff had just won the North-South open at Pinehurst, playing spectacular golf on a demanding course, but Forest Hills gave him a good deal of trouble, and his scores, for some time, were between 70-74—scores which were being matched by a number of local golfers who had learned the shots the course required. Middlecoff finally established a course record with a 63, which he still holds with Mickey Gallagher, Jr. He did not do it, however, until he bowed to the special demands of the course, which meant sacrificing his reliance upon the big drives.

2. *You may be over-experimenting,* so that you are developing fair ability in several ways of hitting the same shot, but excellence in none.

It is possible for a person to become an excellent golfer with over-experimentation, but unfortunately he will be carrying a ghostly millstone about his neck. After a sound swing has been grooved, the function of additional practice should be to eliminate missed shots. If a fundamentally new swing is attempted

for a flimsy reason, it will not lower your score to have two distinct methods of hitting the ball well, just as a person is not a better thinker merely because he can express his thoughts in two separate languages. Harvey Penick made a rather sad admission to me one day. He said, "I know so many different ways of hitting an iron shot that often I don't know which one to use."

Harking back to the matter of "missed shots," it may well be that the chief difference between the golfers in the '30's and those in the '50's is not in the swing, but is rather the result of excessive practice, which gives the moderns a higher percentage of correctly struck balls. When I was playing basketball, I prided myself on my ability to shoot fouls, and often engaged in friendly competition with a friend. We used precisely the same method of shooting, but whoever happened to be practicing the most generally sank the most shots. If one of us had spent half his practice time experimenting with other methods, it would have been lost practice.

Settle on one of the broad golfing methods permanently, then work on increasing your "batting average" with the shot. (One of the best amateurs produced by Texas would not practice anything but completely straight shots.)

3. *You may be improving but it has not appeared in your scores because of the "plateau of learning."* This means that there are often times in learning when improvement has to build up over a period of time before it bursts through to reveal itself in permanently better scores. As Art Wall said recently, "It seemed as if suddenly everything began clicking."

4. *You may be improving but records may be inadequate, or your analysis of them may be in error.* For instance, the more greens you hit, the more putts you will seem to take because you will not be chipping them close to the hole for one-putters.

5. *You may be improving in one part of your game which you are practicing, but gradually losing skill in another part which you may be neglecting.*

6. *You are playing just as well or better as far as shot making is concerned, but course conditions have increased distances, affected the flight of the ball, or affected putting distances or breaks.*

7. *You may be over-practicing something,* such as driving, *that does not show up easily in scores.*

8. *You may be under-practicing something,* such as chipping that does show up easily in scores. Also, the better you get, the more practice it takes merely to hold to the improvement you have made. A great pianist must practice hours each day just to hold what he has. Hence, to *improve* takes even more effort.

9. *Practice has somehow led to confusion.* The best antidote is to lay off for a while and give yourself a chance to forget recently acquired confusing habits.

10. *The new technique may not have been properly incorporated* into serious play. (See "Why Golf Lessons Fail.")

11. *For some reason interest and attention have slackened.*

12. *You may be trying to learn a competing skill at the same time.*

13. *You have found errors in your form and are having to forget old techniques.* This unlearning does not immediately show up in better play, but will eventually.

27th, **SECRET**

How to Eliminate
Stubborn Errors of Form

Many players have a golfing error which seems to defy correction. Often they have been told how to correct the mistake but, for some reason, the error persists. One such error is shanking. Since it is the worst, it will be useful to use it as an example.

Shanking inspires such fear that it will bring about poor performance even if it is only occasional. It is a glaring example of the interaction of psychology and mechanics in golf. Shanking will produce fear, and this fear will then produce more shanking.

I was once caught in this vicious circle while trying to qualify for one of our Georgia tournaments. I played the first nine holes in 39, and the next nine in 57. I was determined to finish the round and that was the only reason I did. I even began shanking chip shots, and finished the last few holes bunting the ball with a wood club. I was so abysmally bad that everyone else seemed free to laugh at the situation. There were a few who were not amused. They were those who had had the same experience at one time or another, and I would not be surprised if some of them had one or two apprehensive moments the next day.

84

After trying many remedies, I finally found a successful one adapted from educational psychology. It has been found that if a typist has a persistent error in the writing of a word, she can eliminate the error by making it deliberately. If, for some reason, she persists in writing "cat" as "cta," the error will disappear if she deliberately spells the word "cta" for a number of times. Peculiarly enough, when she again comes across the word "cat," the letters will come out correctly.

When neither golf professionals nor interested amateurs could help me with their variety of cures, I adopted the above method. I practiced shanking deliberately. It disappeared in a few practice sessions and I never had any more trouble.

Incidentally, this is a fine method of ridding oneself of other conspicuous errors, such as slicing, hooking, etc. *As one practices an error, he gradually learns what accentuates the mistake and what alleviates it.* With knowledge comes confidence, and with confidence fears leave. When fears leave, we are able to get the most out of ourselves.

Some stubborn errors require a rebuilding of one's game. The tendency to shank can very well be the "bug" in a particular golfer's swing. Serious "bugs" of this kind have forced a number of ambitious golfers to scrap a particular method of swinging for an entirely new one. When there is either a major weakness or a number of minor weaknesses, and one has the time, it is best to begin all over again. There will be an initial slump, of course, but this is the only route by which avenues of improvement can be reopened.

With instruction and practice, even stubborn mistakes will be eliminated. If they are not, *it is likely that there is a wrong "fixed idea" behind the error.* If there is, no improvement will occur unless this "fixed idea" is brought out into the open by a sympathetic professional.

If the error has been corrected in practice, it may still not work in actual play because the new method is not properly incorporated into the game. Very often a new technique is introduced too quickly. Results are often worse than with one's old method. This quickly destroys both the confidence of the golfer and the value of the lessons.

In order to avoid such an occurrence, two things should be done. First, the new technique must be over-learned so that even some loss in execution will not be discouraging. Second, the new technique should be pitted against the old—say on alternate shots in practice—until there is no question as to which method is superior.

If the new technique still does not work, further lessons are needed to check on causes. Then back to the practice tee for a repetition of the process. This develops ultimate confidence and a smooth transition that will make it unnecessary to say, "Every time I take a lesson I get off my game"—a rather common frustration.

28th **SECRET**

How to Eliminate
Psychological Errors

We have emphasized the need for practicing to eliminate *mechanical* weaknesses. This also applies to *psychological* weaknesses. The method of handling the matter is the same as that used in removing errors of form.

The first step is to keep a record of those shots which are missed for no apparent mechanical reason—shots with which we normally have no difficulty. These shots are sometimes referred to as "jinx" shots. There are also "jinx" holes. For top-notch golfers, there are even "jinx" tournaments.

A simple method of destroying "jinx" shots is to practice them at the very place they are missed, if this is possible. If it is not possible, a duplicate situation can be arranged on the practice fairway. If even this cannot be done, the shot can be played in imagination. Practice will reveal that it is not the shot which is at fault, but one's own attitude. If the attitude is changed, the trouble generally disappears.

Here is a simple example. For a time, on our number 7, I duck-hooked my drives into a bank about 130 yards in front of the tee. This happens to be the only hole on the course in which a higher tee shot than usual is required. However, a normally good drive will not get into trouble. I knew that psychological factors were producing the missed shot. It happened that my tee shot on number 11 was almost always satisfactory. So I said to myself, "I will play this just like number 11." I had no further difficulty. I could have solved this same problem on the practice tee by *imagining* that I was playing number 7, because peculiarly enough, a jinx will give you trouble even in practice if the attitude to the shot is the same.

Although I solved the problem satisfactorily, I do not consider it a good long-range solution. It would have been better to have learned what my attitude was and what mechanical errors resulted. Had I subconsciously modified my stance? Was I striving for additional distance and allowing the right hand to overpower the left? Was I trying to steer the ball to the left because the fairway over the hill sloped to the right? Was it part golfing attitude and part fear? Is the tee a little slick?

"Jinx" holes often result from "jinx" shots. A "jinx" shot on a given hole will result in higher scores on the hole. If this occurs

enough times, our anxiety spreads to include the hole, or even the course. Sometimes chance produces high scores on a given hole. Instead of being philosophical and realizing that a coin can come up tails three times in a row and that a golf hole can be "messed up" by chance in the same way, we become anxious. This anxiety perpetuates the "jinx" hole by inducing experimentation.

A common psychological weakness is to succumb under pressure. If this occurs often, the best answer is to play under pressure so often that it becomes a natural part of your playing condition. This is the "tournament toughness" of which the professionals speak.

No matter what the psychological weakness, it is just as subject to correction as a mechanical weakness. The answer is always remedial practice.

29th **SECRET**

How to
Come Out of a Slump

There are times when one's whole game *seems* to have gone to pot, and there are times when it *really has*. What steps should be taken then to come out of a slump? Here are the most important:

1. *Determine whether or not you are really in one.* It could be only a statistical variation. If the slump is no greater than those you have hit in previous golfing years, it is best simply to ride it out. Experimentation under such circumstances can well lead to a prolongation of the trouble. False slumps may be due to lack of practice, changes in the weather, changes in the accuracy of the greens, or the fact that your competitors may be riding a wave of good golf.

2. *Revert to a previous form.* A genuine slump often comes from experimentation with a swing that happens to work well temporarily. The experimental form then becomes a habit. Later, the person forgets how he got into the habit in the first place. Nothing will produce a slump faster than a new technique which was temporarily successful and which becomes a "fixed idea." This situation leads us into golfing blind alleys. To get out of them, we must trace the cause of the slump. This will eliminate frustration, and then we can seek out remedies with a clearer mind. An excellent and quick remedy is to go back to the last technique used prior to the experimentation. Return to your standard form and build from there.

3. *Make a shot by shot analysis to see where the strokes are being lost.* Often a slump causes confusion, making a slump within a slump. The golfer says, "My game has gone to pieces." He is so demoralized that he has no interest in practicing. He can't think clearly as to what remedial measures are indicated. The situation is so painful that he may decide to lay off for awhile. This is not a bad procedure, but it can be improved upon.

Generally, the initial loss is on the greens. Poor putting will put a great strain on chipping and both may collapse. It may be that you have had a weakness in your iron play for some time, but that it was camouflaged by good putting and chipping. Your tee shot may be at fault. A gradual loss of distance has so

lengthened the game that you are actually playing a longer course. This frequently occurs if a person has a tendency to fade long shots. Follow up the analysis with corrective practice. The errors cannot cure themselves. At first, single scores will not be better, but the average will gradually rise. Then the occasional good games will inevitably crop up.

4. *Keep and review your notes.* Forgetting can produce slumps. It is wise to take notes of all techniques that have been successful. Unfortunately, because of the human urge for experimentation, we often subconsciously make a habit of what was at first an experimental swing. The previous better swing is forgotten. Notes will help you get back in the lost groove.

5. *Let forgetting help you.* Forgetting can get you into a slump and forgetting can get you out of one. If all remedies fail, it is a good idea to take a rest from the game. You may forget bad habits. Experiments have shown that learning can occur through forgetting *between* practice sessions. The mechanism is not completely understood but it has been noted in maze learning by rats and humans, in tossing rings at a stake, in learning a new series of numbers, and in chess. Some psychologists believe that such improvement through forgetting is due to the gradual extinction of numerous psychological and physical difficulties.

6. *Practice intensively.* You may not be playing or practicing as much as usual. In this case, the solution is obvious, so don't experiment with form.

7. *Clear up outside emotional problems. The slump can be due to emotional factors* that are producing inattention. Such factors can be feelings of insecurity, other types of fear, and problems about which you cannot make up your mind.

It is best for the golfer to believe that all emotional problems can be solved—and they generally can be. Even when they cannot, it is possible to refuse to permit the emotional problem to complicate your life. One great golfer went into a permanent decline because of a marital problem that could have been solved. Instead he brooded about it and never took the steps that were indicated. Another golfer went into a slump that lasted for many months. He thought he had a fatal disease, though he really was all right. On the other hand, the great Babe Didrickson refused to permit her quite serious condition "to get her down," and won great victories when others would have been in justifiable despair. One of the inspiring sights at the Masters is to see Sarazen competing as if he were nineteen, demanding no quarter, and extracting a comparable enjoyment from the game as if to say, "No hungry generations tread me down," if we may be permitted to paraphrase a line from Keats.

30th, **SECRET**

How to Gain Confidence

Golf is a doubly difficult game because you must conquer both physical and psychological problems. One of the latter is how to gain confidence.

Confidence is not something that can be created out of thin

air. No amount of confidence will get a ball into the hole if it is improperly stroked. A scared golfer with a good stroke will not play as well as he can, but he will still defeat the confident golfer who has nothing else to back him up. Psychology cannot overcome physics.

Feelings of confidence are deceptive. For instance, when I was a youngster with only three clubs, I putted with a two iron. I still have great confidence in my ability to putt this way, but I can putt much better with a putter in which I have less emotional confidence but more intellectual confidence. One of the reasons why many golfers don't improve is that they have false confidence in wrong methods.

This has been recently verified by experiments reported in *Science News Letter* of December 12, 1959.

"People Under Stress Do What They Learned First.

"Under stress, we may revert to earlier learned ways of doing things, momentarily forgetting some of our most recent lessons.

"This is the implication of research by psychologists Dr. Richard Barthol of the University of California, Los Angeles, and Miss Nani D. Ku of Pennsylvania State University."

True confidence is not a permanent possession. It will deteriorate in the presence of continued failure. The best method for the development of confidence is to over-learn.

Over-learning leads to successful play. Successful play leads to confidence. Confidence leads to more successful play. Paul Runyan told Jack Murphy, former president of the Southeastern P. G. A., that when he improved his short game so that he felt he could get down in two, his iron and wood shots began going "straight as a string." He was no longer plagued by the fear of missing the green on second shots, and the removal of this fear eliminated the psychological flaws in his long game.

A feeling of confidence is beneficial because confidence and fear do not exist simultaneously, and fear is the great destroyer of shots. Fear is destructive because it tends to activate muscles which should not be used. Fear also tends to prevent movements of other muscles which should be used. This results in shots pulled off line, shots that are hit "fat" and shots that are topped. Fear makes one stupid. Fear will cause you to ignore the computations you have made and, at the last instant, you will decide to "hit the ball a little harder." Fear will cause you to draw back from the ball as you hit it—like the pulled punch in boxing—and the shot will fall short. In short, fear is generally disastrous. The cocky, unafraid player has the advantage, unpalatable as this idea is to most of us. Sometimes the "cockiness" is concealed, as it should be, but it is nevertheless effective. This cockiness is, more than likely, the difference between otherwise equal players and accounts in large part for those golfers who are better than their equals when there is pressure.

Cockiness is better than fear but it has weaknesses of its own. In the Southeastern P. G. A., played at Augusta in 1959, misplaced confidence turned a sure birdie four into a bogey six. An excellent professional three-putted from a distance of about three inches! The pin was in the hole. He rapped the putt firmly. It struck the pin and bounced back to the same position. Rapping the ball smartly again, he announced, "That can't happen again." But it did. The moral is that absolute confidence is no guarantee of success. To be cocky without cause is better than to be fearful without cause, but both attitudes are faulty, since they are unrealistic and do not conform to the true facts. The best attitude in the long run is to be as coldblooded a calculator as possible with no self-delusions. The best antidotes for fear in golf are first to over-learn, and then to do what you fear until you become accustomed to it.

31st **SECRET**

How to Handle Anger

What about temper? In the 1945 Dallas Open, played at the Dallas Country Club, one of the leaders hit a phenomenally long drive on number 3, a sharp dog-leg to the left, par 4. His ball carried to about the 245-yard marker and, from the tee, it appeared that it was headed right for the green. The golfer strode up toward the center of the fairway, but did not see his ball until a spectator said it was in the rough to the right of the fairway. The ball had received an abnormally bad lateral kick from a hard depressed spot on the fairway. The pro was obviously disconcerted as he examined his next shot. The ball was under a mesquite tree; neither his swing nor the flight of the ball would be affected. It was an open and simple shot with a wedge to the green about 85 yards away. But his second shot went into a trap. He still had a simple explosion to the cup. Now the ball barely came out. He wound up with a five. This bad hole started a series of bad holes and he very quickly was out of the running. It all started with anger.

First of all, those who wish to control anger must *give up the feeling that they are "entitled" to become upset*. Once a per-

son feels that he is "entitled" to gripe at bad luck, the elements, a baying dog in the distance, or even his own incompetence, the battle is nine-tenths lost and the golfer must forever fight being a golfing emotional cripple. Griping is first "justifiable" for major items, then "justifiable" for lesser disturbances, and finally it becomes a senseless self-destructive habit. To avoid such a disintegration of the golfing personality, it is best to give up the idea that you are justified in any anger.

Second, *if you make this decision, you must practice continuous self-control.* Since the time of the great Sigmund Freud, it has become the almost universal belief that if we repress or suppress anything it is automatically bad. The more I practice psychology the more I believe this to be erroneous. In the ordinary pursuit of our daily affairs, we exercise considerable repression. We do not spontaneously embrace strange people in public places merely because we like their looks. We do not steal in a department store merely because we don't have enough money. We go to great lengths to train children not to wet the bed or to move their bowels in public. In fact, the whole process of making the transition from child to mature adult involves continuous repression. On a number of occasions when patients have had persistent depression from dwelling on unpleasant thoughts, or when manic patients became unusually excited by stimuli that should not have disturbed them, I have found that training the individual to suppress helped when nothing else would. No doubt the suppression of legitimate and realistic impulses *can* lead to trouble, but we must believe that, as a fundamental principle, suppression is neither good nor evil, but depends on the particular circumstances.

Use every opportunity to become upset as an opportunity to practice "not getting upset." It will take time, but this can be learned like any other game.

Third, for those who are not able to train their intelligence to govern their emotions, there is a way of channeling anger.

Direct the feeling into a resolution for practice. Punish yourself with remedial practice. The more times you become angry, then, the better your game will get. Every missed shot thus produces its own correction.

Anger that is misdirected can cause trouble, but anger in itself is not bad. The stimulus toward improvement would very well disappear if it were possible for a person to train himself not to react at all. As a matter of fact, there is some question as to whether a person could learn to play golf unless a bad shot was a source of discomfort. In studies of the learning process, it has been found that a response that is followed by unpleasantness will get weaker. If it were possible for us to train ourselves to become completely undisturbed by a bad shot, learning would not occur.

The best attitude to have toward the game, then, is to practice self-control so that useless anger is not permitted to develop, and useful anger is directed into a quiet but completely determined resolve to remove golfing flaws through remedial practice.

This throws light on a matter of common observation. People who play golf on a narrow course hit straighter shots than those on a wide open one. Shots which arouse no unpleasant feelings on a wide course are quite distasteful on a narrow one. The continuous "noxious stimulant" acts like an electronic device to stimulate constant correction. On an open course, this would be lacking.

The above explains, in part, the psychology behind the common belief that your golf will improve if you play with good golfers and become worse if you play with poorer. With high handicap golfers, your fair shots will look so good by comparison that you will be pleased and learning will not be stimulated. With better golfers, even your fair shots will not be good enough. This will be unpleasant, and can stimulate improvement.

The above implies that for the very good golfer to become

better he must set up his own higher standards, and set them so high that there will be unpleasantness attached to the shots that even good golfers would consider good enough.

32nd, **SECRET**

Beware of
Golfing Masochism

A person who derives a perverse pleasure from self-injury is called a masochist. Some players tend to be golfing masochists. Some break golf clubs. Others will deliberately cost themselves additional strokes.

A very fine golfer hit his second shot into water in front of the green on a par 5. Instead of moving up to the water's edge and lobbing the next shot to the hole, he perversely hit several more balls into the water from a range of about 250 yards. By a narrow margin he failed to place among the leaders, and this cost him an invitation to appear in the Masters the following year.

Another form of self-destructiveness sometimes operates among those who seem to lose their touch if they find themselves in the lead. Their attitude may change in a number of different ways but it all winds up with the same result—defeat. An over-confident person may take foolish chances or become careless. Another may feel free to experiment. A shy person may wonder, "What am I doing here?" I know a very nice professional who does this. He tries to disappear.

Strange as it seems, just as there are golfers who are completely determined to win, there are others who subconsciously prefer to lose. These are sometimes the ones who appear to be blowing up. Others appear to be perennially "unlucky" because of a perverted desire for self-punishment. Some just quit, and some treasure the reputation of being "good losers."

To play any shot in such a way that all one's ability is not used is self-destructive. Be on guard against such golfing masochism. It is not enough, however, to be forewarned against possible golfing masochism. We need to know what to do about it. As Socrates pointed out 2,000 years ago, no one knowingly injures himself. On the surface, he may *appear* to be doing so, but inside he thinks that everything he does is really to his best interest. I have found this to be quite true of those with suicidal impulses; these impulses disappear when the patient is made to realize that it is not to his best interest to kill himself. The loser who persistently fails to measure up to his demonstrated abilities sometimes is found to believe that it is better for him to lose than to win. If the problem is important enough to the individual, it would pay him to consult a good psychologist. This is the type of problem which clears up almost immediately when the thinking underlying it is exposed.

33rd, SECRET

How to Develop
and Harness Compulsions

In order to become skillful at anything, the great requirement is persistence. In order for persistence to maintain itself, emotional drive is necessary. Some people have more of this drive than others. Some have it so highly developed that they are possessed by the drive instead of possessing it. One form this takes is that of the compulsion.

A compulsion can become pathological and senseless when patients feel that they can ward off evil by not stepping on the cracks in the sidewalk or when golfers become superstitious, or it can be harnessed into productive channels. A harnessed compulsion often leads to spectacular achievement. I have had compulsive patients who were only passably bright make straight "A" marks.

Whenever I have wanted to complete a task that appeared to be arduous, I have deliberately made a compulsion out of it. This is the simplest way I know to provide maximum insurance for success. A compulsion is not difficult to understand if we think of it as a very powerful interest. Any interest can become

compulsive. The more we do something, the more interested we are in continuing it. This is true of the hardest and most menial of tasks.

I read recently of a barber who had become nationally famous and wealthy as an after-dinner speaker. He still continues to barber!

During the depression, there was no work available. Under the WPA program, an unemployed street sweeper received a weekly relief check. He bought a broom and swept streets for nothing.

During World War II it was found that captured doctors would collaborate in cruel experiments on fellow prisoners if only they were permitted to practice medicine.

In such cases, we must suspect that interests had become compulsive. The trick, then, is to harness proper compulsions.

A proper compulsion can be generated by first overcoming inertia, then establishing correct habits of practice, and finally making these habits so strong that they drive us automatically to learning. It is said of Hogan that he has often practiced in bad weather. By this manner he prepared himself to handle the special variables that surround play in rain, wind, or cold. It is also likely that his habits were so strong that he could not keep from practicing even when the weather was bad.

The compulsion must be controlled, for it can lead to the error of the "fixed idea." This is a common underlying error which perpetuates poor form when a golfer adopts an idea so strongly that it restricts his ability to make alternative decisions.

One instance of this occurred in the 1954 Masters. Billy Joe Patton, the long-hitting amateur, had decided before teeing off that he would not play it safe but rather would "go for broke" along the route. With some excellent play and some luck, he came to the final round leading the field with a few holes left. At this point his lead was such that he could have won the tournament with conservative shooting. Playing with the attitude he had carried with him throughout the tournament, he elected to play for a birdie by gambling with a long wood to reach a par five hole in two. He put the ball into the water and lost to Hogan and Snead by one stroke.

Another instance occurred in the Ryder Cup matches in 1959. On a water hole, when the American team and one British player had missed their second shots, the British team would have won if the final player, Weetman, had played safe. (They were one up with one to play.) Instead, Weetman shot into the water, resulting in the loss of the hole and tying up the match. When he was questioned about the costly mistake, Weetman said, "The only way I know how to play golf is to always shoot for it."

Fixed ideas—no matter what the source—often lead to persistent errors. In giving lessons, the professional would be wise to stimulate the learner to give expression to such ideas.

There is only one good fixed idea: *do what the situation calls for*. The problem is to develop a useful compulsion to improve but to guard against trying to solve all problems with one solution.

34th, SECRET

How to Practice
Golf Thinking

At the 1959 Masters Tournament, Hogan stated that he was hitting the ball as accurately as he ever had, but was not doing as well with his "thinking," since he was not playing much tournament golf and had not been practicing this phase of the game.

A reporter said, "But, Ben, I thought once you learned how to think in tournaments, you always knew how to do it."

Hogan shook his head and said, "No, you have to practice golf thinking just like you practice shots."

I have often thought the pre-game warm-up, as practiced by the professionals on the circuit, could be improved upon if it combined both a mental and a physical warm-up. Jones has proffered the advice that one should get his mind on the game prior to going to the first tee. Hogan has advised practicing golf thinking, but it is presumed that he was referring to practice rounds. The idea occurred to me recently that probably the most efficient warm-up would be to play the course in imagination, practicing in succession the very shots a particular course demands. If I were a Demaret, therefore, or any comparable

golfer, preparing to play the Augusta National, I would hit in practice the type of tee shot which would be required that day on No. 1. As soon as I was satisfied, I would practice the probable second shot, and so on around the course as far as I cared to go. This would provide a physical warm-up, give one practice in making a transition from one club to the next in the probable sequence demanded by the course, come close to duplicating the precise shots that would be demanded, and give one some idea of his immediate strengths and weaknesses so he can capitalize on one and finesse around the other.

Strokes are lost in almost every round played because of poor golf thinking. In my own case this accounts for one-fourth to one-half of all the strokes I lose during a round. Golfing friends who shoot in the low seventies estimate they average a loss of three strokes a round because of making mistakes when they "know better."

A rough estimate of the number of strokes lost by failing to think straight about shots in a round—or strokes that can be saved by good thinking over lackadaisical thinking—are:

$$
\begin{array}{rcl}
75 \text{ shooter} & - & 3 \text{ strokes} \\
85 \quad '' & - & 5 \text{ strokes} \\
90 \quad '' & - & 8 \text{ strokes} \\
100 \quad '' & - & 12 \text{ strokes}
\end{array}
$$

Strokes lost because of poor thinking will reveal themselves in:

1. "Jinx shots."
2. Badly judged distances.
3. Strokes lost on poor gambles.
4. Experimental shots.
5. Forgetfulness about how to hit the shot.
6. Hurried shots.
7. Failure to observe the "bite," "roll," or "break" of your opponent's or partner's ball—particularly on chips and putts—wind, pin position, etc.
8. Unnecessary tension.
9. Unnecessary reliance on the caddy.

There is only one way to remedy "thinking" weaknesses. After each round of play, you must list all the missed shots attributable to poor thinking. This will alert you to the need of concentration in this area. You will find that thinking errors tend to repeat themselves, just as mechanical errors of shot execution reoccur.

For instance, on a green where your approach putt runs a good bit past the hole, you will find that you will *generally* be long.

On holes where your wedge shot will not bite, you will repeatedly run too far.

On holes on which your drive tends to be a smothered hook, you will tend to continue to smother-hook.

After you have determined the source of thinking errors, you must set up a duplicate situation and practice the shot until the correction has been made. The best way to do this is at the very spot on the course where the error was made. Often a few shots will be sufficient, since we are supposing that the person actually has the shot in his bag. If it is not possible to make the correction on the course, it can be done on the practice grounds by playing the shot in the imagination.

Here is an instance of how good and bad thinking can affect the golf game of a duffer. It happened in a handicap Calcutta tournament in which the prizes were substantial. The person who bought the duffer happened to be playing with him. The duffer had difficulty breaking 100, but as he came into number 17, he was leading the field by 7 strokes. He was some 12 strokes below his usual score because his partner had made him use his putter whenever he came within 70 yards of the hole! Unfortunately, the duffer was in the trap on 17 and, as his partner was walking away toward his own ball, he sneaked out his wedge, and flew the ball over the green into the marshes, for a fat 7. He blew up on the last hole to drop to third place.

The brain acts very much like an electronic computer. First the facts must be fed into it; then it gives directions to the muscles to produce the answer to a golfing problem. Hogan has always tried to feed as many facts as possible into his brain prior to making a shot. For years he advocated that this be done between shots prior to reaching the ball. In effect, this gives one an opportunity to feed more information to the "computer."

Thinking is so important to golf that the person who actively practices thinking will have the advantage. There are some who are "excited" by thinking and actually play worse when they do it. These people find it useful to play quickly. Psychologically, however, they are under a handicap.

One way of insuring golf thinking is to get into the habit of first itemizing the factors to be taken into consideration. When the computer has come out with the answer, execute it without regard to your own or others' feelings about the matter. Don't let your emotions trick you out of the right answer.

I was witness to such a "trickery" a few days before writing the above. An experienced professional and his amateur partner were leading the field in a P.G.A. tournament. On the 17th hole, the pro had a six-foot putt for a birdie. He was in front of the hole, with the grain running from right to left. His partner, a local player who knew the greens well, told him that the grain was very strong and that he should allow more for it than usual. His decision was to putt two inches to the right of the hole. At this point the caddy said he should putt it straight. He then decided to "split the difference." He missed it. It made a difference of $500 in prize money. He said later that he knew that his original calculations were right, but he had foolishly overridden himself.

The emotions are the deadly enemy of the thinking process, and even an electronic computer can be at the mercy of them. When Harry Truman and Tom Dewey were running for the presidency, a computer was used to attempt to predict the results of the election. Political scientists worked for months gathering and feeding to the machine the information it needed to come up with a prediction. The computer came up with the prophecy that Truman would win. However, this answer did not fit in with the personal conclusions of the statisticians, with the way other polls were running, and with the way early returns were pointing. So the operators of the machine, no doubt emotionally motivated by their desire to prove the value of computers, fed it enough other material to show that Dewey would win. Truman won.

Don't permit emotions or impulses to override calculations. In otherwise equal competition, the emotional player has no chance against the cool, calculating one. To become a "calculating one," calculating must be practiced. Hence it would seem unwise to give up chances for such practice by continually asking the caddy's opinion.

35th, **SECRET**

Make Universal
Out of Particulars

It has been said that the mark of the thinker is one who can develop universals out of particulars. Applied to golf this would mean that if we discover something about hitting particular shots, our learning can be made more useful if we can express it as a general rule.

For instance, our principle of "eliminate variables" makes it easier to determine the value of techniques we may wish to try. Another "universal" or generalization on a particular course could be "all putts break toward the river." The more such generalizations a golfer has, the easier golf thinking becomes.

A practical application of this comes to mind in respect to the apparently unpredictable breaks on the old putting greens of the Augusta Country Club. Some said they had been putting the greens for 20 years but still couldn't figure them out. Others tried to memorize as many of the breaks as possible. One golfing group even went so far as to make liberal use of the "trial run."

In order to make order out of nonsense, two club members dropped a circle of balls around the hole on each of the greens. From this it was discovered that in almost all cases the ball broke in an exaggerated manner either to the north or the west. Although this generalization did not help on every hole, it improved their ability to read the greens.

However, we cannot rely entirely on generalizations, unless we adopt another generalization: generalizations are only guides. One must consider whether there are particular conditions that modify the generalization. Otherwise, generalizations will become dangerous fixed ideas.

36th **SECRET**

How to Destroy
Your Golfing Delusions

In golf we must often be on guard against ourselves. We think we are doing one thing when actually we are doing something else. We can have images of our golf swings which do not conform with the facts. We tend to believe we have excellencies which do not exist. Sometimes we believe we have deficiencies which are not there, and even change a swing that is all right to begin with.

For instance, a number of golfers have advocated that the arms be held as closely together as possible. An aid to doing this is to keep the elbows together. Hogan's description of the position is that the arms are pressed together as if held by a sheath of rubber. This seems theoretically sound to us since it tends to remove the variable of loose arms.

Several years ago I read of this need to keep the arms pressed toward each other with the pit of the elbows facing upwards. I tried it but my swing became constricted and I lost distance. When I showed a friend what I had been doing and what I was now doing, he said that I had been doing it right the first time.

To correct your golfing image, the best bet is the advice of a teaching pro. Movies can help some but are not quite as good. Someday devices will be available that will give us a truer picture of ourselves, but until then we must rely a great deal upon the ability of others to see us as we really are.

37th, **SECRET**

How to Handle

a Gambling Shot

All golfers are faced with situations in which they feel a risky shot should be tried.

Assuming that the need for the gambling shot is clear—the so-called "calculated risk"—what then can be done to give it the best chance of being pulled off?

First, the chances are much better than average if the shot is preceded by what might be called "the surge of confidence." With this, one experiences an almost overwhelming feeling that a given shot can be made. I have experienced this myself a number of times in various sports. It is followed by success that defies the law of averages and seems to approach the impossible.

An Augusta physician tells me that some twenty years ago at

the Masters, Gene Sarazen was walking down the 18th fairway when he and the others noticed a crow on the limb of a tree about 40 yards ahead. The crow was facing the other way. Quick as a flash, Gene dropped a ball and pulled an iron out of his bag, and before anyone could realize what had happened there was a flurry of feathers as the ball caught the crow squarely in the seat. Gene must have had the surge of confidence!

I had a similar experience not too long ago. I was hitting eight iron shots on a practice fairway. To the left of the green there is a tall forked pine. I pulled a shot that went through the narrow fork. There were several spectators and one said, "Well, that won't happen again in a thousand years." I had the surge of confidence, and saying, "Not in a thousand years?" dropped a ball and put it squarely through the fork.

How this feeling develops, I am not sure, but one thing I know. There isn't a trace of anxiety or fear in it. No extraneous muscles will jerk at the wrong time when this feeling exists, and the ball has the best possible chance of receiving a maximum effort. At these times, if the gamble is indicated, fire away. You'll probably make it if the shot is in your bag at all.

If the feeling is not there and the shot still has to be played, be deliberate and think the shot through. Even though you must gamble, try the shot which has the most chance of success. This eliminates experimental shots. A well-thought-out shot can inspire confidence, for if you settle down properly to the ball you will suddenly feel right; right feelings accompany right action. This "feeling right" helps to insure a successful gamble.

There are major and minor gambling shots. One of the minor (although cumulatively important) ones involves the decision of when one may permit oneself to aim for the flag and when one should aim for the green. As a general rule, it is best to aim precisely where you wish to go. Your ball has a better statistical chance of going where you are aiming than to any other spot.

In golf, if the problem is simply a question of "win or lose" there is no option. The pin must be shot for. However, there are many situations, particularly in medal play, when the question is strictly statistical. Often the problem can be solved by asking yourself, "Are my chances of gaining a stroke equally as good as my chances of losing one?" If a four can be made by hitting the green in two on a par five, and if a six will be made by missing it, nothing will be lost or gained over the long pull by always shooting for it. This, however, presupposes a knowledge of the pattern of one's shots, since the golfer would need to know if he could hit such a target half the time. For this reason, it is wise in practice to leave the practice balls on the ground periodically after hitting them, to obtain some knowledge of how well grouped the balls are around the target. Knowing your normal pattern of shots, simply place it over the target point, in the mind's eye. Then, if your chances of gaining a stroke are about the same as those of losing one, shoot for it. This is a general rule that can be applied to many situations, but would need to be modified at times by other circumstances.

At the Texas Open one year, Ben Hogan was in a trap to the left of the green on a par five. He surveyed the break of the green, and asked the caddy to hold the flag. He blasted. The ball took a break. The caddy took the flag out and into the hole went the ball for an eagle. He could not have made it if he had shot for the green in general.

On those occasions when, because of hazards, one cannot safely shoot at the flag, the target must be an artificial one in the center of our superimposed pattern, but even in this case aiming should be precise. The ability to aim can only be developed by aiming.

There are persons who become tense if the target is very precise. Such persons may come up with an abnormal swing because of anxiety, and hence would do well at the moment to have a less precise target. However, psychologically we would have to consider this a weakness, and the ambitious golfer would be obliged to work to remove it.

A great danger in the gambling shot is that it tends to set up a state of anxiety. Much depends on the result, and this preoccupation with the result will generally destroy the golfer's ability to execute the shot. If you are using a putter in a trap, you are anxious to see if it will run up the bank and are apt to half-top it. If you must shoot through a narrow opening in trees, you will be tempted to pull your head up prematurely to see where the ball is going. On a delicate chip, you may not complete the swing. Hence, to insure a higher percentage of success, a marked effort at self-control is required. Deliberately complete the shot before you examine the results.

38th, SECRET

How to Avoid the Most-Missed Shots In Golf

An excellent rule to follow during serious play is never to hit an experimental shot. Of all the shots missed by golfers, this is probably the most costly.

Shots that vary from the norm are generally those during which something new is being tried; or they may be modifications of normal shots. For instance, on number 8 of the Augusta

National, one contender on one occasion, and another contender on two occasions, pulled their tee shots close to the woods on the left. From this position, to hit the green on this par five, both would have had to hit hooked second shots. On each of the three occasions the shots were pulled too far to the left, ruining chances for crucial birdie fours and producing bogies instead.

Even the mildly experimental shot is dangerous. Here are a few of the reasons:

1. The experimental shot has its own "bugs" with which you are not familiar, and therefore would not be as safe as one in which the "bugs" could be taken into consideration.

2. The experimental shot requires considerable concentration. This additional focus of attention is very apt to cause the player to ignore management or other factors such as wind, breaks, etc. The experimental shot will actually be a form of distraction.

3. The shot cannot be hit with confidence and, even if the experimental stroke is actually an improvement on one's old method, there will be an element of anxiety that will generally do more than neutralize any theoretical advantages.

As we see, the experimental or non-standard shot adds variables and hence should be a shot of last resort only.

What can we do if our shots suddenly begin to sour during a round? If we continue to experiment, further flaws may develop. The safest method of correction is to assume that some experimental technique has crept into our game. Very often we can recall exactly when we began trying this different thing. Whether we can recall the cause or not, it is a good idea to revert to whatever form was used just prior to our having trouble.

If the flaw is not prominent, it is best to allow for the error for the time being. Jones did this in a crucial round of a tournament that he went on to win. He had developed a noticeable fade. He simply allowed for it and corrected it later.

The overcoming of one's urge to experiment during a round is a difficult thing and few can accomplish it completely. If one does, he will eliminate many otherwise unexplained misses.

Another large group of shots consists of those that are missed because you have been unnerved by your own or someone else's shot. One of the very best practical psychological suggestions to be made by any player on this subject was that of Walter Hagen. This champion was justifiably famous for his competitive spirit and was unfazed by missed shots. In the 30's I saw him play in an exhibition match at Gainesville, Florida. On a course he had not previously seen, he shot a 72. On at least four holes he made pars after great recoveries from missed shots.

Hagen's suggestion was that even a good golfer should assume that he will make some errors in every round. This attitude is an excellent antidote for golfing panic and, for that matter, for anxiety or fear in general. In the treatment of psychological ailments, the probing process is generally emotionally painful. Often patients will wish to avoid appointments. This problem does not come up as frequently if the patients are told in advance that many sessions will not be pleasant. Another problem is that progress is seldom continuous. A patient has many relapses, but when he is told in advance that they will occur, he will take them in his stride. Physicians have found that, in painful examinations, pain is withstood much better by the patient if he knows it is coming.

Forewarning, then, is excellent for aborting anxiety. An equally good variation of Hagen's method can be used in match play. It is best to assume that your opponent will halve or win some holes with very fine or even lucky shots. This will prevent you from being unnerved and you will not react by missing shots.

Always, when any shot is missed, the immediate psychological task is to retain a positive attitude. Let us take the case of your missed drive which winds up some 150 yards from the tee. This can be recovered by going for the green if it is reachable. However, on many holes this cannot be done. Suppose we proceed to hit toward the hole and then survey conditions. You are now a very short shot from the green. As a matter of fact, if you were at this spot in "one" rather than "two," more than 100 yards ahead of your opponents, you would expect your chances of getting a birdie to be very good. With this attitude it is much easier to get the ball close for an actual par than to brood about the fact that you have already lost one stroke. I think it was Middlecoff who pointed out that on holes of equal difficulty, one known as a hard par 4 and the other as any easy par 5, more fours will be made on the par 5 than on the par 4. This coincides with my own experience, and illustrates the effect of attitudes on one's shot-making ability.

Positive thinking or realistic optimism can be developed for every conceivable golfing situation. If it is practiced conscientiously at every opportunity, you will have reserve psychological forces ready to come to your rescue whenever the going is rough. If you do not practice it you can get into the habit of being overwhelmed by a poor shot or an unlucky one. If you are overwhelmed, you have become so because you have not practiced the art of realistic optimism—that is, optimism based on the favorable elements of a situation.

39th, **SECRET**

Computing Distances

Many golfers judge distances subconsciously. They look at the hole and "feel" the distance. This is not as accurate as consciously computing how far you are from the green. The "feel" can be made much more accurate if it is helped mechanically and psychologically. This is particularly true when you are within pitching distance of the green.

The soundest method seems to be that of Jones, which involves the control of distance simply by shortening the grip on the shaft. If you will drop balls at one-yard intervals back from the green for about 100 yards, you will find that you can control the length of the shot by simply holding the club at spots higher and higher on the grip. With this mechanical method Jones was then free to concentrate on direction. The balls automatically were close to the hole if he computed the yardage correctly.

Gauging the distance involves certain psychological factors. *Hitting* the ball the correct distance is a psychological horse of another color. In order to practice hitting precise distances, I had Harold Lamb, our greenskeeper, calibrate all distances from our practice green 100 yards back. Whenever I hit practice balls I did not play shots from one position, but scattered them at yard intervals from the green on back. I noted my finger position on the grip at each distance. On the course, the sole problem was to estimate the distance, hold the grip at the point indicated for that yardage and pull the trigger.

I find that if I break up the distances to the flag into intervals of ten yards, yardage can be gauged precisely. This is fine for short distances but is difficult to do for distances over 100 yards. Distances up to 60 yards are easily handled. When the distance is greater, I move to the side of the ball, estimate where the halfway mark is, divide this into yardage, multiply it by two, and that is it.

Of course "feel," or the subconscious, is still important, but even this can be developed consciously. A general rule which should guide us in the development of "feel" is always to use muscles which have the greatest potential for touch. Proper muscles can build a physiological fence around the shot and prevent bad judgment.

Practically speaking, this means that your estimate is more accurate if the more sensitive muscles are used for the shorter distances. You must avoid using a yardstick when a ruler is needed.

The most delicate touch is in the tip of the index finger; then the other fingers, wrists, forearms, arms and body. Smaller muscles are more sensitive discriminators than larger ones. Also, if few muscles are used, the additional variables that accompany the moving of many muscles are eliminated.

I was recently able to correct a flaw in my irons that plagued me for many years. I seldom missed hitting the ball, but the blade was not straight at contact and I missed greens on both sides. I finally struck on the idea of utilizing the sensitivity of the ball of the left thumb. By concentrating on its position, I improved my ability to sense where the blade was. (On theoretical grounds, the use of the sensitivity inherent in the index finger of the right hand should aid in putting touch.)

Since all shots do not require equal amounts of touch, there comes a point at which strength becomes a factor. Otherwise, what is gained in touch is lost in accuracy if, for instance, the club is loose in the hands.

The right combination of distance and direction can only be achieved through varied practice. There are additional factors such as wind, bounce, and temperature whose influences need to be appraised. The simplest method of appraising is just what you would now expect—practice and play under as many different playing conditions as possible.

40th, **SECRET**

To Save Strokes,

Avoid Ego Involvements

Ego involvement is a Freudian term having to do with what is generally known as pride. We are ego-involved when we use a three iron when we should be using a two or even a wood club. One of the secrets of the phenomenal play of Paul Runyan was that he didn't allow his ego to affect his choice of clubs. If his opponent used a six iron, Runyan would not hesitate to use his four wood if the situation called for it, and tales of his accuracy with such shots are legendary.

Ego involvements affect other golfing situations. We may play an opponent "even" when a handicap is indicated. We may elect to shoot over a dog-leg instead of around it. We may turn in a lower qualifying score just to get into a higher flight, or we may turn in a higher qualifying score in order to insure winning a trophy in a lower flight. We may use a high-compression ball because very hard hitters do, although we could get more distance with less compression. We may turn only good scores into the handicap committee for the prestige of a low handicap, and we may turn in poor scores for a higher handicap that will help us win a trophy. We may shoot for the pin when our general accuracy can only justify shooting at the green.

There are some ego involvements which can be beneficial, such as pride in improvement; but, in general, ego involvements cause us to become unrealistic. This prevents us from doing what a golfing situation calls for, and thus is disastrous. Nothing can be solved if pride produces wishful thinking or otherwise prevents us from seeing the problem as it is.

41st, SECRET

To Think
or Not to Think

We have emphasized the need for conscious thinking, but a great deal of golf is played *subconsciously*. The upper levels of thought do not have a great deal to do with the actual execution of the shot. The chief functions of upper-level thought should be used *prior* to hitting. Brains make themselves felt more in learning the most effective methods of practice than in guiding an infinity of muscles through a detailed conscious maneuver of final execution.

To use an illustration from music, the greatness of pianist Vladimir Horowitz is not a brilliant interpretation rendered before thousands in Carnegie Hall. Horowitz achieved greatness by first intelligently riding herd on muscles and tendons hour after hour. When performance night came, the muscles and tendons did the work. Of course, Horowitz' conscious mind focused on what he was doing. His thoughts were ahead of the music his fingers were playing for him. Yet even this thinking was not as conscious as one would suppose, for it had been practiced and, having been practiced, it took care of itself.

127

You cannot do too much thinking prior to the shot but you can do too much during its execution. Thinking that hasn't been practiced out can very well introduce a variable and thus spoil the shot. What we have here is really "experimental" thinking, which has the same type of "bugs" as the experimental shot.

Ralph Guldahl's decline as a golfer has been attributed to too much thinking. When he was at the peak of his golfing powers, he was asked to write a book about the technique of the game. In his hotel room, he would write awhile, then pick up a club, check his grip, stance, and elbow position, and write some more. By the time he finished his book, he confessed that he had developed such an acute consciousness of the process of hitting the ball that he had lost his touch. We are reminded of the old story as to how Santa Claus developed insomnia. Someone asked him if he slept with his beard under or over the blanket.

Snead has advocated avoiding thinking. Betsy Rawls, who has a degree in physics, states that she leaves tournament shots to be taken care of by the subconscious. Bob Jones seems to have summed it up best, years ago, when he said that he limited his concentration to the very last improvement he had incorporated into his swing.

The question of thinking or not thinking has intrigued me for some years, and when I was trying to solve the problem, I tried an experiment worth reporting. I had concluded that I was not leaving enough of the execution of the shot to the subconscious. I thought, "Well, I'll crowd out golf thinking with extraneous thinking." I finally hit on the idea of singing during the execution of the shot. Late one afternoon, I went to the Northside course in Austin, Texas, and during each shot I sang "Home on the Range." My caddy laughed, until I started to play! I came in with 32—my best nine-hole score to that time!

I could not wait to get back to the course the following afternoon after work. Score—42. The trouble, I decided, was that I had learned the song so well I could sing it and worry about the execution of the shot at the same time!

To sum up: thinking that involves the actual *execution* of the shot should be done in practice. The actual golf management and thinking that goes on in the *planning* of shots cannot be overdone during play.

42nd, SECRET

Taking Off the Pressure

It is a matter of common golf knowledge that "pressure" generally results in higher scores. We recognize that most of us do not play as well in tournaments as we do in casual golf. Too often practice rounds prior to a tournament do not give us a good clue as to who the winners will be.

The reason for the higher scores is the addition of psychological variables. These psychological variables are not generally present except under tournament conditions. Since most of us do not participate in many tournaments, we have the fear that generally accompanies action in an unknown area. We play a worse game than we are capable of playing. Those who are "tournament tough," but who are no better golfers than others, come much closer to their normal scores.

Some golfing gamblers have taken advantage of this by making bets that are larger than their opponents are accustomed to. The story is told of a football coach who was also a good golfer. When he was winning his matches, the pressure would naturally be on his opponent, and there was no problem. When he was losing, he would keep on "freshing" the bets and would inevitably recoup on the final holes or hole.

On one occasion, he had a short putt for a par on the final hole. His wealthy opponent had one several feet longer. Considerable money was involved in the bet. Unfortunately, his opponent sank his shot and the coach missed. When another golfer commiserated with him about the tough luck, the coach was silent, then slowly said, "No, it wasn't tough luck. I just outsmarted myself. I've been so much in the habit of betting this way that I overlooked one thing. I forgot that my big bet meant so little to this man that there was no pressure on him."

During the depression, when money was hard to come by, a golfer used a system which kept him consistently in the winning column. On one occasion he and his partner finally won $2.00 (after being in the hole for $54.00) under nip-and-tuck conditions that left them exhausted and trembling. He decided to try to eliminate future pressure by gambling in small amounts within the limits of the money he won. A bank account was set up and, when he lost, it was paid out of this fund. His winnings were deposited. This took the pressure off the betting. In addition, since he played regularly with the same group, it was easy for them to handicap each other so that net playing ability was equal. For added insurance, he practiced for about thirty minutes a day between playing days. From then on he was not affected by the pressure, and built up what was, for those days, a sizable winning fund.

Here are general ways in which pressure can be reduced:

1. *Over-learn.* Learn any golfing skill to a higher degree of skill than you need. Pressure will cause you not to perform as well in play as in practice, but you will have enough skill in reserve so that the pressure won't show.

2. *Do not "fresh" bets when you are losing.* To paraphrase Newton again, "a person who is losing will continue to lose and a person who is winning will continue to win," generally speaking. Let your opponent be under the pressure of recouping losses. Of course, this situation must be assessed each time. If he has gained the advantage through performance and luck much beyond his average skills, it is safe to "fresh," although, at most, this will only make for an even bet.

3. *Practice pressure play.* There is more than one kind of pressure, so one must subject himself to each in order to develop immunity. Match play, medal play, tournament play, etc., all have their own special pressures. Continuous play under each type will gradually immunize you.

4. *Never play a careless shot.* If a person will adopt the attitude of never playing a careless shot—no matter what the circumstances—the tendency to succumb under pressure is lessened. Pressure shots are often missed because the need for being careful adds a psychological variable to the player who is thoughtless in informal play.

5. *Do not expect to play better than your average golf.* As your golf records will show, the laws of probability will determine your score. If you try to do better than you can do, it will introduce an additional emotional variable and you will play a worse game than usual. It is best to let the score take care of itself. Otherwise, you may shoot a poor score on a day when you might normally be destined for a good one. You cannot prevent the appearance of scores either better or worse than your average if you simply let the laws of chance or probability take over. As the old saying goes, "If you didn't bring it with you, you won't find it here."

It has been said, "A hungry pro is hard to beat," implying that the pressure of having to win to survive will cause him to play better. This does not necessarily follow, since this pressure constitutes an additional variable and is likely to cause him to come apart at the crucial moment.

In medal play, it is not a good idea to think in terms of what has to be shot to qualify or win, except in special circumstances in which gambling shots are clearly indicated. There is no psychological advantage in concentrating on a final score. As a matter of fact, this is a disadvantage, since instead of concentrating on the best possible method of executing the individual shot in accordance with good golf management, we give ourselves an additional variable to think about which exerts a distracting influence.

A better attitude to have when one is playing medal golf is to think of a round of golf as a string of pearls. To have a good string, one needs a series of good individual pearls. The emphasis then should be not on the final score but rather on concentrating on stringing together as many well-thought-out shots as possible. If you are successful in doing this, the score will automatically be low. When Capablanca, the great chess master, was asked how many moves he saw ahead, he replied, "One." So don't allow a long-range objective to interfere with the immediate golfing job at hand—"to hit this shot facing me the best I know how."

If our string of pearls does happen to have some flaws, the flaws may still be fewer than those of our golfing equals if they saddle themselves with unnecessary pressure caused by scattered concentration. If it happens that we lose because more of our pearls are faulty than those of the winner—we can always go back to our pearl-repair spot—the practice tee—and fashion some better ones.

The great problem in tournament play is to avoid those improper psychological attitudes which cause golfers to play worse than they generally do. Amateurs particularly are apt to be affected by the odds and, if they are playing against someone who is "doped" to win, they tend to blow up. At the peak of Bobby Jones' career, the newspapers played up the idea that it was "Jones against the field." This put most of his opponents in a very uncomfortable psychological attitude, particularly in head-on play. They were half defeated before they started. Fortunately for them, Jones had a weakness of his own. He played best when he was under an apparently painful tension. When he thought the golfing situation was well in hand he found relief in more relaxed play, and then generally played his worst golf.

A good pre-game attitude to have when playing those who score either better or worse than you is not to be concerned with the outcome of the match at all, but to focus all your concentration on individual shots—to shoot your average game only. If you are satisfied to shoot your average game, you will likely do so. *Against equal players in match play this is generally enough to win* since no psychological variables are introduced by you, whereas your opponent is very likely not in the same frame of mind. If he is a somewhat better player, the chances are almost fifty-fifty as to whether you will shoot better or worse than your average, and you have an equal chance to make an even match of it. If he happens to be off his game, your average score will be enough to win easily. The psychological situation is similar to that of a person who must swim a long way to shore from a sinking boat. It would be best not to think about what the final result might be. In such a circumstance, it would be better for one to concentrate on his stroke, and the manner and frequency of his rest periods, leaving the result to itself. Anxiety is a common cause of drownings, and it is also a common cause of lost golf matches. Both disasters occur because of too much concern with *results*.

While we are on the subject of removing pressure, it might be apropos to discuss the use of chemical means of controlling tension. Both alcohol and tranquillizers are to be avoided, although many good rounds have been played under their influence. The general objection is that their effect is temporary. They also tend to lead to addiction and will prevent you from computing properly. Finally, if you are aware of a golfing problem, these chemicals will cause you to ignore your computations.

One of the long-range dangers is that you can become conditioned to playing your "best" game only when under their influence, and eventually, as you deteriorate with the "whiskey fingers" that polished off one of our great golfers, you can play neither with nor without the stuff. Except for emergency cases, the psychological route is much safer and more effective.

Golfers are people, and all the things which affect people affect golfers. A disastrous psychological habit which has driven many patients to despair is to be plagued by unpleasant thoughts. Since this is a problem of many golfers in circumstances too numerous to mention, it might be helpful to outline three effective methods which can be used to take care of this particular psychological condition.

First, deliberately suppress the thoughts which are disturbing. With practice this can be done as Scarlett O'Hara did in *Gone With The Wind* when she said, "I will think of that tomorrow."

Second, crowd out distressing thoughts with mental or physical activity of a somewhat extraneous nature. This is a method that I suspect Patton and Snead use in their give-and-take with the gallery.

Third, make a deliberate effort to think as many optimistic and pleasant thoughts as possible.

43rd, SECRET

How to Apply the Pressure

There is only one way of applying pressure to your opponent in head-on play—through your golfing ability. Any form of direct or indirect needling should be restricted to the golfing group in which the relationship is so close that the usual amenities are relaxed.

The proper attitude should be that the game is more important than the player, and that the players are more important than the outcome of one's personal matches. The written rules should be upheld; beyond that, golf is a game for gentlemen and requires an extreme consideration for others.

Some years ago in the National Open, Bobby Jones, while addressing his shot, drew away from the ball. He then re-addressed and struck it. When the hole was completed, he had apparently parred it. He called a stroke upon himself, however, because as he had set his club for the second shot, the ball had partially turned. The stroke permitted Willie McFarlane to tie. In the playoff, Jones was defeated. As long as golf is played, this example of sportsmanship will not be forgotten.

135

This calls to mind, by contrast, what many consider to be the grand slam of golf stories. Two golfers came to the 18th tee all even. John hit his ball straight down the middle. Harry sliced into deep rough. Both caddies and players looked for the ball for almost five minutes, after which time Harry said, "Well, you all go on. If I don't find it in a minute, you can have the hole."

John and his caddy had barely got to their ball when Harry yelled, "I've got it." He played a great shot that landed on the green. John turned to his caddy, "You know, that son of a bitch is going to beat me yet, and I've got his ball in my pocket!"

However, within the rules and spirit of the game there is often opportunity to apply a psychological pressure which may be the deciding factor in a match or tournament. Some opportunities occur now and then, some are always at hand. Here are ways in which this can be done:

1. *Become an expert on putts of five feet and under*. If your opponent is uncertain on such shots, his game will often collapse. This, of course, is a limited objective. Even more pressure can be exerted by a general excellence in the short game.

2. *Defeat a golfer in his own golfing department if possible*. A long hitter becomes disconcerted if he is out-driven. A good putter gets wobbly if someone else is matching his skill in a department where he expects to have an advantage.

3. *Defeat a golfer in his own psychological department*. Some years ago in a club championship match play tournament, I was warned by members to be on guard against my next opponent. He was a very strict rule-caller, and used the rules as an obnoxious psychological weapon. I brushed up on the rules in advance and was aided by a nice stroke of fortune. On the first hole, when removing his ball from casual water, he replaced it in a way that improved his position. We had a polite and lengthy discussion about this immediately, finally deciding to

leave the decision to the professional when we came in. However, this did not prove to be necessary, since his game promptly broke down. Peculiarly enough, he was quite friendly after this and assisted me in a minor financial venture.

In another match in the semi-finals of an invitation tournament in Texas, I was defeated by an opponent who, after hitting a ball out of bounds, used the "duplicate ball" trick. He had a hole in his right pocket through which he would drop a ball to the ground. It is almost impossible to see the trick in operation. "Here it is," he said, and that was the match.

I had occasion to play him again in another tournament. This time I told my opponent, "Mr. G—, you know they've got a lot of local rules here and we don't know them all. Suppose we play improving the lies everywhere—no out of bounds, and no other penalties." There was an odd expression on his face but he agreed. It was a fair match this time but, unfortunately for a good story, he beat me again.

4. *Present him with the "fait accompli."* That is, shove a good shot in his face and let him do better. It was believed that Bobby Jones would sometimes hit a drive deliberately shorter than his opponent in match play in order to hit first. When he played his next shot on the green or close to the hole, the pressure of the *"fait accompli"* was on his opponent. Deliberately hitting a shorter drive than one's opponent could develop into a comic affair, however, if *both* golfers knew the maneuver. We might even see the first drive hit with a wedge!

Gene Sarazen has been suspected of deliberately putting his second shot in the trap to disconcert his opponent and excite the galleries with his deadly explosion to the flag.

Paul Runyan demoralized Sam Snead in the finals of a P.G.A. tournament by hitting first to the green—often with a wood when Snead was using short irons—then finishing him off, 8 and 7, by sinking the putts. Of course, Runyan did not create this particular opportunity, but it illustrates the general principle.

It may well be that my opponents have, on occasion, disconcerted themselves. In a poker game in which I was fortunate, one player said later to the rest, "I should have known better. He was reading my mind."

On another occasion, my opponent had been kidded by his friend when he learned that he was pitted against a psychologist. On the first tee, he whispered, "Don't let him talk you out of it." I hit first with a fair tee shot. He hit rather poorly. I, of course, said nothing. My opponent's friend leaned over and said to him, "Tricky bastard, ain't he!"

5. *Play the "two more."* The term "two more" is an English expression for the tactic known in this country as "making it hard for him." It is the *"fait accompli"* presented to an opponent after you have had to lose a stroke. Here is an example:

You are playing a par-four hole. You dub the tee shot. The next shot is critical. You play for a safe bogey five. Your opponent's second shot must hit the green to win. The pressure is on him to capitalize on his chance. The hole is "won" but it is not yet won. If he doesn't get on, he will not win the "won hole." Even if he does get on, you may have hit a good third shot and put it close. If both of you are on with little difference in your shots, you can continue the "two more." If you make your long putt, you have probably saved the hole. If you put it close, he has to avoid three-putting. If he puts his ball to within three feet of the hole and you do not do quite as well, you can still "make it hard for him." If you drop your four-footer, his three-footer will become psychologically longer.

There are many opportunities in match play to capitalize upon apparent disaster. Although the statistical advantage is against you, the psychological advantage will be on your side if you put continuous pressure upon your opponent to win a hole he has theoretically won or to win a match that seems to be just about closed.

The principle of the "two more" in match games is akin to that of "keep the ball in play" in medal golf. Those who are pursuing the leader are in a psychologically advantageous position. By simply keeping their ball in play, continuous pressure is exerted. The leader must do the very difficult thing of winning what has already been "won." This, in effect, is an additional psychological variable, and is worth several strokes to those who are pushing him.

44th **SECRET**

Do Not Rationalize Failure

An ominous obstacle to improvement in golf is the habit of rationalizing. When a person rationalizes, it means, to put it simply, that he places the blame for his defeats upon outside persons or circumstances. This protects his ego by taking the sting out of failure. It turns painful depression into less painful anger. It tears others down and, by this tearing down of others, seems to raise him in prominence, much like the last survivor of a battle royal who looks like a giant in the ring if everyone else is on the floor. It is bad psychology to rationalize.

First, *it is a most unpleasant personality trait*. The least desirable companion on any golf course is the constant griper. It

is a mark of selfishness to impose on others the necessity for listening to this bilge.

Second, *the tendency to excuse one's game hinders remedial learning.* No improvement is possible unless the individual takes full responsibility for all his golfing errors and proceeds to correct them.

Third, *even if rationalization removes the sting from poor shots, it retards learning.* Learning is faster if we attach a painful reaction to a poor shot. When you rationalize, it makes failure more easy to take and thereby makes it harder to learn. Rationalizing or the making of excuses does not inspire remedial practice. You do not realize that remedial practice is necessary because you do not accept personal responsibility for the error.

Fourth, *it is not wise to rationalize even when there is a good basis for it.* If you do, it will intensify feelings of hopelessness, and prevent you from attaining a satisfactory level of performance.

Even gross physical handicaps should not be used as excuses. Cruickshank, Armour, Nichols, Martucci, Furgol and others have made names for themselves under the greatest of physical handicaps.

45th **SECRET**

Be Realistic about Putting

Putting is the most difficult part of the game. If one is not realistic in this regard, he will fail to take the steps which will bring about improvement.

Putting is difficult because it is highly complicated, fully as complicated as three-cushion billiards—and perhaps more so. In fact, Willie Hoppe, who mastered billiards, was astonished that he could not overcome his poor putting. This is not too difficult to understand. His table was small; greens are large. The table was absolutely level; greens never are. The cloth on the table was always of the same speed; greens vary almost from hour to hour. He played on one table; a golfer plays on 18 different greens. Hoppe played in a calm atmosphere; in golf, the weather can change from cold to hot, calm to windy, dry to humid, etc., in a matter of minutes. On the billiard table skill generally wins; on the green, luck is often decisive. In billiards there is virtually no problem of grip, stance, stroke, or type of cue to be used; in golf, the variations are almost endless.

Although we are aware of the danger that this emphasis on difficulty may affect the very confidence which is reputed to be essential for good putting, no progress can be made unless we first face the facts. Even if there is some lessening of confidence at first, this will be better compensated for by relying more on putting practice than by believing that wishful thinking will cause putts to drop. My own experience has been that the more I tried to generate false feelings of confidence, the more careless I became, and the more putts I missed. In fact, I seem to make many of my long putts at unpredicatable times—probably because of the laws of chance.

After we accept the fact that putting is a difficult art—a game within a game—it is much easier not to be discouraged. If we know a trip will be long, it is much easier to accommodate to it than if someone says that the journey is a short one and it turns out not to be so. In addition, when the difficulties are overcome, our competitive position is much safer than it would be if the difficulties did not exist at all.

46th, **SECRET**

The Place
of Confidence in Putting

Year in and year out, the average golfer will miss about the same percentage of putts. However, there is considerable variation from day to day, and from week to week. Many golfers say, "I am putting well," or "I am putting poorly," when nothing other than chance is operating.

The mathematical truth is that it does not make much difference whether the putt drops or not on any given occasion. With any consistent amount of practice combined with any given method of stroking, the so-called poor luck and good luck will balance out over a period of time. If the stroke becomes better and if you practice more, the average will improve, of course, but poor luck and good luck, like the poor are always with us. It is essential that the golfer believe this. If he does not, the resulting experimentation will introduce variables, destroy confidence, and effectively block improvement.

Confidence is a "sometime" thing. On the days when one putts well, confidence grows automatically. On other days, confidence droops. Confidence is secondary. Confidence does not produce good putting. It is good or even lucky putting that produces confidence.

The only confidence that is worth anything is certain knowledge of how much skill you do have. This comes from much practice and periodic analyzing of records to see where you stand. Any other type of confidence is false confidence, as anyone can attest who has practiced excessively indoors and attained great confidence, only to find that the putts would not drop on the course.

Confidence can only continue to exist where there is a limited and attainable objective. No matter how good a putter one is, the further he is away from the hole the less confidence he has, and rightly so, for this is what experience has taught him.

What is the answer then? As always, it is the learning and practice of better methods. This automatically gives one confidence at greater and greater distances from the hole, until we get to the point at which confidence again fades.

The best confidence, then, is confidence in the value of putting practice.

47th, **SECRET**

Touch versus

Direction in Putting

As you may have concluded by our past discussion of putting, the great difficulties with this part of the game arise from its many variables, some of which are not subject to our direct control, such as course conditions. There are two variables that do come within our powers: speed and direction. Anything we can do to improve our ability to gauge distance or to increase accuracy should be done. Unfortunately, by taking measures that improve direction we often injure our touch for speed. The big undecided issue in putting has always been whether to emphasize the mechanical adjustments that accentuate touch or those that help guarantee direction.

Should the grip be firm or delicate? Should the wrists be unyielding or broken? Should the ball be stroked or tapped? Should the blade be light or heavy? And there are many other questions. The answer to the problem of putting form is generally decided by copying whatever player has the current reputation of being the best.

There may not be a hard and fast answer. In the short putts, for instance, accuracy is at a premium. Our chief concern is that the blade will always meet the ball at the same angle. A firm grip, firm wrists, and arms that do not wobble eccentrically are indicated. We must deliberately sacrifice touch for accuracy.

In the longer putts touch is at a premium, for in most cases a three-putt green results from balls that are too short or too long, not ones that are off line. Our chief concern is distance gauging is to use the grip and muscles that will produce the maximum touch. This indicates a looser grip and smaller muscles in order to capitalize upon the inherent greater sensitivity of the fingers of the right hand, particularly the index finger. We must deliberately sacrifice accuracy for touch.

Although putting in itself is difficult enough, it would seem that for the perfectionist there is no alternative but to use varying styles of putting according to the "logic of the situation." Putting situations have great variety; hence it would seem that the next advance in putting technique will have to come from the abandonment of the idea that one stroke suffices for all shots.

The right combination of the light touch versus firmness comes about through variety in putting practice. In order to achieve this variety, it is recommended that you scatter a number of balls around the hole in the form of an ellipse. This will give practice with the grain, against the grain, downhill to the right, downhill to the left, etc., at varying distances.

An important variable to be removed in putting is not hitting the ball squarely. This variable can best be removed by practicing long putts—the longer the putt, the greater the observable distance between the well-hit putt and the slightly mis-hit putt.

If only short putts are practiced, the difference between a well-hit putt and a slightly mis-hit putt is hardly detectable.

One of my golfing companions who had been sold on the idea that "if you can make the short ones, you don't have to worry about the long ones," never practiced anything but 3- and 4-foot putts. He was quite accurate with these, but rarely made a long one. Of course, if my friend had conscientiously practiced weaknesses, he would have split his putting practice time to provide for remedial practice of long putts.

48th **SECRET**

The Truth
about Carpet Putting

The chief value of practicing on a carpet is to standardize the grip, stance, and stroke so that the ball will roll straight. This is best undertaken on a uniform rug so that our observation may be more accurate.

Carpet putting should be practiced only until you are reasonably sure that the swing will "repeat," as modern lingo says. It will also be of value for sinking short and uncomplicated putts.

However, there are comparatively few uncomplicated putts, and the more difficult ones must be learned on the greens.

It is only by practicing on greens that one learns to putt on greens. Remember, "no transfer of training."

In this connection, an experiment was performed by the

writer that is pertinent. At a time when his putting was "off," he purchased a putting device, which was ingenious in that when it was placed six feet away on the average rug, the ball could be putted across the rug, up a short inclined plane into a hole. If the putt was either missed or made, the ball would be returned. Practice results were as follows:

First thousand	493 sunk
Second thousand	604 "
Third thousand	737 "
Fourth thousand	795 "
Fifth thousand	915 "

In the last thousand shots, the putting seemed very good. Runs of 30 and 40 consecutive shots weren't rare. Only four putts were missed out of the last 100. It was apparent that he had become one of the world's great putters. There was only one thing wrong—he was no better on the golf course.

The reader will already have guessed how this came about. This type of practice violates our rule that practice is faulty to the extent that it does not exactly duplicate the thing we wish to learn.

All that the writer had learned was how to make a six foot putt on a perfectly level rug, with no pressure to affect the outcome, with no distracting influences, with no need to change the stance, to gauge the distance, and to notice the direction closely!

Harvey Penick spotted the trouble immediately. The wiry nature of Texas greens is such that putts will kick off line unless they are stroked with over-spin. The writer cut his putts. On a smooth rug with a set distance, it was possible with a great amount of practice to putt well, but it did not transfer to the greens. The reverse is also true. Putters who could out-putt me on the greens were not as good on a carpet. But the stroke Penick taught me, which was more successful on the greens, could not compete with my cut putts on the carpet device. In time, it might have.

Putting on a carpet may actually hurt one's putting. Some of the bad habits which develop from it are:

1. It weakens the habit of paying attention to distance.
2. It weakens the habit of paying attention to slopes.
3. It weakens the habit of concentrating to eliminate distracting influences.
4. It weakens the habit of being careful about grip and stance.
5. Since we are apt to do more putting on a carpet than on the greens merely because of the availability factor, we may over-learn bad habits.

Let us contrast what happened when I practiced the same number of shots on the putting green.

First thousand	381	sunk
Second thousand	308	″
Third thousand	373	″
Fourth thousand	372	″
Fifth thousand	393	″

In the five thousand putts on the carpet, I rather quickly reached a point at which little improvement was possible. After five thousand putts on a green, there was no apparent improvement.

After years of experimenting with carpet putting, I have reluctantly come to the conclusion that at best it may not be worth the effort, and at worst it is a competing technique that will confuse the golfer and slow his progress.

49th SECRET

The Psychological Putting Stance

There is a considerable emphasis in golf literature about the need for keeping the head still. Many people have gone so far as to advocate, "Knock the ball out from underneath the eyes," *i.e.*, not moving the head until the ball is well on its way. Some have said that if the ball rolls true for the first six inches, you won't have to worry about the rest. These people have advised selecting a target just that length ahead of the ball. This may indeed be well for short putts when accuracy is the sole consideration, but it is unsound psychologically for any others. In order for conditioning to take place between the strength of the stroke and the length and curvature of the putt, the ball must be observed while it is rolling. Thousands of such immediate observations ultimately and subconsciously develop "touch" for both direction and green-reading. Hence, the stance of the putter must be open enough to enable the player to follow the roll of the ball without moving his head. Since man is incurably curious, I am afraid that closed stances have a tendency to induce head moving. Its vogue is more than likely due to the

150

fact that with such a stance it is easier to put top spin on the ball. The player aiming at putting perfectionism would be wise to use a compromise stance. In the long-range development of your putting, aim at a putting stroke and stance that combine an open stance or view enabling the eye to follow the ball with a stroke that gives over-spin.

50th **SECRET**

How to Use

Finesse Putting

It is a difficult thing to make the muscles do something they are not trained to do. A common experience of the spectators banked around the 18th green at the Masters is to watch player after player run past the cup on the downhill putts. On the other hand, let the greens be slowed by rain, and many of the golfers will putt short. At the end of the round they can be heard to say, "I just couldn't make myself hit the putts hard enough, after remembering how fast these greens have always been."

Muscles seem to have a brain of their own. They want to do what they want to do even if you are trying to tell them the opposite. This is particularly true in the short game. In such cases, it is best to finesse the muscles.

Clarence Mobley, one of the very good putters at the Augusta Country Club, finesses his muscles on fast downhill putts by striking the ball with the toe of the club rather than with the "sweet spot." He then strokes the ball as firmly as he would otherwise. He is very accurate in judging speed on these putts.

Another method of finessing is to use a different stroke for different types of putts. On the difficult downhill putt on a fast green, one of our scratch players hits the ball on the down-swing. This apparently gives the ball "drag" and counteracts the green speed. He is very good at this putt.

On an uphill putt against the grain, most of us cannot force ourselves to hit the ball hard enough. One professional golfer who handles this problem very well tells me that he changes from a shoulder stroke to a wrist stroke, one that he normally uses when chipping. By this means, he achieves the finesse. We do not yet know enough about putting to indicate what strokes are best for various shots. It will take experimentation. If golfers would begin to pool their knowledge about specialized putts, we could have a genuine improvement in this area.

Finessing is generally indicated when we know what the shot requires but cannot force ourselves to do it. On the greens, such situations occur when we habitually do not allow enough break, run past the hole or fall short of the hole. The general principle to use when finessing is to substitute a mechanical method for a psychological one. Changes in stance, grip, putter, or stroke should be considered.

There are some occasions when the finesse can be psycho-logical. A change in attitude by the use of the imagination, such as I indicated for jinx holes, is sometimes effective. On a fast green, for instance, it is difficult to combine the two ideas of hitting the ball with authority and not hitting it too far. This generally causes confusion, and the shot is apt to wind up short because of the indecision, and may the next time be hit too hard. I have found that I can handle this situation if I imagine that the hole is closer to me than it really is. Then I putt firmly to this imaginary hole. The faster the green, the closer I imagine the hole to be. I do the reverse of this when the greens are unusually slow. In general, however, it is safer to trust to mechanical rather than psychological finesses. Each golfer should search for those that suit him best. The finesse principle can also be applied to shots other than putts, particularly when course conditions are unusual.

51st, **SECRET**

Putting Slumps

and What to Do about Them

There is no more demoralizing condition in golf than to be in the throes of a putting slump. When the putting is bad there develops a chain reaction which can cause a general blowup. If our short putts are not going down, we make a desperate effort to get the long putt or chip so close that we "can't miss." This adds a pressure variable that brings about flubbed shots. Next we make a great effort to steer our iron shots so that they will land on the green. This results in pushed and pulled shots which make the short game even more difficult. Finally, we try to hit the drives so far that the iron shots will be so easy that we won't have to worry further. This pressure variable weakens the drive by upsetting our usual timing. The result is golfing chaos. What can be done?

All of the methods which we have previously advocated for coming out of a general slump apply to putting slumps. In addition, there are special factors involved in putting which bear closer examination.

First, there may be no slump. In this case the putting is not really worse and hence no changes should be made. The "slump" may be due to some temporary forgetting by the muscles. A voluntary or involuntary layoff is the usual cause of this condition. Such golfers returning to play should not change any of their golfing techniques—no matter how poor the results —until they have practiced enough to regain the touch which deteriorated because of lack of practice. Generally, this touch can be regained rather quickly.

A delusion that one's putting is worse often comes about when course conditions change temporarily. I have noticed that when the greens are in poor shape, many golfers go into a frenzy of experimentation with form and putters. As they do so, their putting goes into a further slump, and this slump will persist even when the greens return to normal, for they now have new techniques which have "bugs" they are unfamiliar with, and these techniques are not as well-learned as the older ones.

False slumps are produced when we do not have objective records of how well we actually are putting and under what conditions. Also, we are apt to misjudge the situation when we play with generally poor putters, or good putters who have deteriorated. Our standards of comparison are relatively affected and we don't know where we stand. The best measure is how we compare with our own past performances, and this requires records.

Second, the slump may not be genuine because it is a temporary statistical variation. There are times when a coin is repeatedly tossed and only "tails" shows up. With putting, nothing but misses can occur at these times. Examine your records and you will find that this type of "slump" is a regular occurrence. It should be sweated out philosophically.

Third, the slump may not have been a true one to begin with but is now. The slump was originally perhaps just an off day or days. Excessive experimentation then produced a genuine slump. Go back to your old form, and stick with it indefinitely. You cannot prevent the averages from swinging back to normal.

Fourth, the slump may be genuine and, in addition, you may not be satisfied to return to your old level of performance. In order to achieve results, you must combine better form with greater practice. The realistic way of doing this is to seek out a teaching professional who is an excellent putter, and model yourself after him. From then on, persistent practice will accomplish the task. If you relapse, you can always return to your model to iron things out again.

To obtain and maintain high putting skill, one must recall the competitive element in golf. To putt well is not enough. You must putt better than others. You must be willing to make the sacrifices that others cannot or will not make.

Gross muscular skills are easily remembered, but the finest skills of muscular learning require indefinite polishing and are quickly forgotten—almost from one day to the next.

Fine singers, pianists, violinists, and billiard players must practice three or four hours daily to maintain and improve their skills. Those who wish any particular degree of skill in putting, must pay the equivalent price in practice. Any other attitude is unrealistic and unproductive.

52nd, SECRET

Longer Drives
and How to Get Them

Very often, the biggest factor preventing a person from obtaining maximum power is his psychological attitude. If this attitude is not a proper one, he puts an artificial limit on his distance. Since there is a good correlation between one's distance and one's over-all play, he thus also places an artificial limit on his scoring averages.

The first requirement for obtaining greater length is an understanding of the fact that very few golfers attain their maximum effective distance, and that it is not likely that the reader has. Some day we shall have a test that will indicate the maximum distance for each golfer, but until that time we must believe that there is a good bit of difference between how far we *do* hit and how far we *could* hit the ball.

The second requirement for greater length is an understanding of the theory of golfing power. The mechanics of generating power have been so well described in other sources that it would be inappropriate to deal with it in detail here. However, it is psychologically helpful if we understand the theory of the power swing.

156

Power becomes cumulative in the correct golf swing—somewhat as it does in a four-stage rocket. In the rocket, the first speed is generated by the burning of the lower end of the rocket. When the rocket is making all the speed it can with this energy, the second stage adds its burst of speed. Then the third stage adds its power. Finally, the fourth stage (in the golf swing, the hands) capitalizes on all the other speeds and adds its own.

It is obvious that no single application of power can do the cumulative job of all four, and it is also obvious that if the stages of the rocket go off in the wrong order, speed must be lost. The part of psychology in this is rather small, but that small bit is important. You must have a proper image of how the power is theoretically applied before you can get out of yourself all that is within you. The greatest single cause of the loss of power is the lack of a proper image of golfing mechanics. "Hitting hard" is not enough. A small golfer who applies his power correctly can out-drive a larger one who does not.

The third requirement for distance is exercise of the will to hit. Many golfers do not obtain the distance they should because they do not hit the ball as hard as they can. Somewhere along the way they found a method of hitting the ball more squarely by hitting it easily. This produced the common golfing delusion that you can hit a ball just as far by hitting it easily as you can by hitting it hard. Those who have made this "discovery" or have picked it up on hearsay are convinced that they cannot hit it hard and squarely. They lose the will to hit hard. This becomes a habit, difficult to overcome.

One reason for the difficulty is that as soon as a "soft" hitter begins trying to use more power, he adds a variable and begins to miss the ball. To hit a ball *easily* and *squarely* is quite different from hitting it *hard* and *squarely*. The latter requires a completely new set of attitudes and learning habits. This relearning produces a temporary slump which will cause many golfers to return to the "soft" hit. In fact, golfers who can hit a shot hard and straight will have difficulty hitting the same shot easily and straight. For power then, the golfer must exercise the will to hit and then learn how to apply it mechanically.

The fourth important requirement for distance is a proper image of how the ball should behave in flight. The best trajectory has an angle of 11 degrees. Many golfers go for years sacrificing distance because they accept a trajectory that varies greatly from this angle. Even worse, many become reconciled to a high cut shot, the greatest distance-killer known to man after the outright dub or shank.

The fifth requirement for those who have the innate power to hit the ball is an avoidance of the confusion of long individual drives with long average drives. A 250-yard drive on number 1 is effectively cancelled out by a hook into the woods on number 2. There can be so much concentration on the single long balls that one forgets the greater importance of longer average drives.

This form of self-destructiveness is caused by ego involvement. The long belter becomes emotionally attached to the "oh's" and "ah's" of his friends and is willing to sacrifice the pleasure of a good score for temporary admiration.

The sixth requirement for gaining distance is avoidance of the attempt to get distance with straightness in a piecemeal fashion. One golfer says, "First, I will learn to hit it straight and then I will hit it hard." A second golfer says, "First, I will learn to hit it hard, then I will learn to hit it straight." Of the two, the second is more apt to eventually wind up with a long straight shot. But even this method can be improved upon. A third golfer who concentrates from the beginning on the long *and* straight shot will come out soonest with the longest straight drive. This involves the psychological principle of learning by wholes rather than parts—a method which is generally advantageous.

Golfers who concentrate first on learning to hit hard or to hit straight are both in danger of having their game disintegrate when they try to put the two pieces together. This will occur because old tricks of timing will have to undergo readjustment.

The club will be moving faster or slower. Old muscles will be given new tasks. The whole natural feel is changed, arousing anxiety. This mental conflict is sufficient to demoralize learning. Slumps and discouragement generally follow, and the golfer tends to return to old inefficient ways, blocking long range improvement. Out of all this have grown the well known observations, "He hits it a mile, but you never can tell where it's going," and "He hits it straight, but he just won't hit the ball."

The seventh requirement for obtaining additional yardage is good tee-shot management. This is not open to most of us, since it is all that we can do to keep good drives in the fairway. It is a factor, however, with good players. Even with lesser golfers, the best spots for drives should be selected more or less in advance, so that the effective average drive will not be reduced by a poorly planned, though well executed, shot.

The eighth requirement for probable additional yardage is experimentation with club-head weight, club weight, length of shaft, and stiffness of shaft. No formal research has been done in this area that I know of. I have done some experimenting and have been able to lengthen my tee shot some twenty yards by the use of shafts which have varied from 46 to 50 inches, and which, peculiarly enough, have given me greater accuracy.

There is a shaft length and club weight which is just right for each individual golfer. This variation is much greater than it is generally considered to be. A slow but strong swinger, such as I am can get more leverage and hence greater speed with longer shafts. A very fast but weak swinger would be at the other extreme and could do better with shorter and lighter clubs.

The ninth requirement is a slower backswing. The disadvantage of the fast backswing is that it introduces additional variables. The faster the backswing, the greater is the force necessary to keep the swing stable. Newton's law of physics, that to every action there is an equal and opposite reaction, gives us the explanation. The faster we swing back, the greater the force that is necessary to keep our golf position under control.

The slower backswing will increase distance in two ways: first, it will simplify getting the club head into the proper slot squarely; second, there is a certain amount of energy burned up in the fast backswing that should be used for hitting.

The tenth requirement for distance is a type of ball that suits one's swing. Not everyone can get maximum distance out of the high-pressure balls. Also for winter play, it is an advantage to use a ball-warmer. A ball travels best at 87 degrees. At 40-50 degrees, a ball will be appreciably shorter. Finally, there is an advantage in using a new ball, and one with a record of uniform compression. The advantage may be only a few yards per shot, but this advantage is multiplied by two on long holes.

The final requirement is sufficient driving practice to keep muscle tone at a good level. This does not require very many practice shots. It is the experience of most golfers that the tee shot requires the least amount of practice.

53rd, SECRET

The Final Secret

In psychology, much use is made of the psychological test. The ideal test is so constructed that individual questions and problems range from the very easy to the very difficult. Some questions can be answered by almost anyone. Some problems can be solved by almost no one.

In this respect, golf as a game is an ideal test. There is a place for every degree of skill, and we can spend a lifetime at the sport without learning it all. This is not a disadvantage. If we were to list the characteristics of a great game, one of them would be that it could not be completely mastered. Golf has this and virtually all of the other requirements needed to qualify as ideal. It is probably the greatest of the outdoor sports, as chess is probably the greatest of the indoor games.

Golf and chess are rather similar. Both have histories lost in antiquity. Golf may well have been brought to Scotland with the invasion of the Romans, who had a similar game, pagano. Both golf and chess are very complex. One man's lifetime is inadequate to exhaust their possibilities. Both games present

problems to be solved by the individual, providing wide opportunities for self-competition. Along with these similarities, both
have a beauty all their own.

We come then to the essence of the final secret. It answers
the question which the reader may have asked himself throughout the development of the ideas in this book: "Is golf worth
the effort?" The answer, beyond which a psychologist cannot
go, may be summed up with: "Golf, like music, love, and art,
has the power to make men happy."

INDEX

INDEX

171